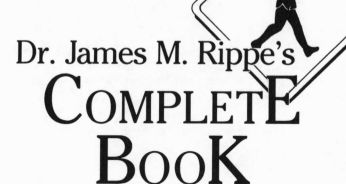

Dr. James M. Rippe's
COMPLETE
BOOK
OF
FITNESS
WALKING

James M. Rippe, M.D.
and
Ann Ward, Ph.D.

PRENTICE
HALL
PRESS

NEW YORK LONDON TORONTO SYDNEY TOKYO SINGAPORE

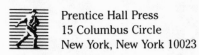 Prentice Hall Press
15 Columbus Circle
New York, New York 10023

Library of Congress Cataloging-in-Publication Data

Rippe, James M.
  Dr. James M. Rippe's complete book of fitness walking / James M. Rippe.
  Bibliography.
  Includes Index.
  1. Walking—Health aspects.   2. Physical fitness.   I. Title
RA781.65.R53   1990
613.7'176—dc20   89-30465
                                                          CIP

ISBN 0-13-156134-0

Designed by Stanley S. Drate, Folio Graphics Co., Inc.

Produced by Rapid Transcript, March Tenth, Inc.

Manufactured in the United States of America

10   9   8   7   6   5   4   3   2   1

First Prentice Hall Press Edition

Dr. James M. Rippe's

COMPLETE
BOOK
OF
FITNESS
WALKING

To America's walkers,
who understand
that even the longest journey
begins with a single step

CONTENTS

PREFACE

For nearly all my forty-one years I have had a deep personal commitment to exercise, including skiing, tennis, weight lifting, karate, and windsurfing. For the last twenty-five years I've been especially committed to walking and running. There has never been a time when I did not exercise, because I have always believed that being physically active makes me feel better and produce more.

As a child, adults told me I was athletic, so I was convinced I could excel in sports. I played varsity basketball and baseball in high school and was a swimmer in college. But this was not the norm among my classmates. In the United States, only about 15 percent of school-age children are told they are athletes and encouraged to participate in organized sports. For the other 85 percent the implication is clear: Sit down and watch television or do some other sedentary activity. Sadly, the message carries over into adulthood and affects the lives of many Americans.

My message is different. I believe that Americans can and should be physically active. Sometimes I see the results of my proselytizing right outside my window. Every day on my way to work at the University of Massachusetts Medical School, I drive past a quarter-mile track in Lake Quinsigamond Park. This is where we have conducted much of our research for the Rockport Fitness Walking Test™ and the Rockport Walking Diet. Now, regardless of the time of day or the weather—at six in the morning or seven at night, in rain or fog—people are walking laps on that track and around the park. They are "fitness walking." I feel very proud that the work we have done at the University of Massachusetts Exercise Physiology and Nutrition Lab has helped people take control of their own health.

People who walk regularly believe they can control what happens to them. They have what I call an inner locus of control. They are much more likely to take charge of their lives than people who don't believe they have inner power. Such people think that their own motivation has a big impact on their health, and medical research strongly supports them. In fact, they can do more for their health than a physician can. To me, one of the most exciting aspects of the fitness-walking movement has been observing millions of people in the United States adopt this inner locus of control.

It gives me great personal satisfaction to know that my lab has aided in dispelling feelings of helplessness. I became aware of this recently when we were conducting an experiment in walking and weight loss involving about eighty people. At the end of the study a woman named Sally who had lost a considerable amount of weight came up to me and said, "I just want to thank you for giving me back my life." I was so touched that tears came into my eyes, but I explained to her, "You gave yourself back your life."

Many people have difficulty understanding that most serious and widespread diseases, such as heart disease, obesity, and osteoporosis, as well as mental illnesses like anxiety and depression in part grow out of daily activities. People who have an external locus of control, who believe that an outside force like a doctor or the government controls their health, won't change their lifestyle to reduce health risks. Several years ago a survey asked people if there was anything they could do for themselves to avoid getting cancer. An astounding 50 percent of adults felt cancer was an act of God, and that they could do nothing to prevent it. They thought this despite nearly a quarter of a century of public warnings against smoking cigarettes and more recent admonitions against staying too long in the sun. Medical research indicates that 35 percent of cancers could be eliminated if everybody stopped smoking cigarettes; staying out of the sun between 11:00 A.M. and 2:00 P.M. and following a proper diet would eliminate another 10 to 20 percent.

In our experiments at U Mass Medical School we have seen how the feeling of control a regular exercise program gives people spills into other areas of their lives. I often ask my cardiac patients to give up things they have enjoyed doing for a long time, like smoking cigarettes or eating eggs for breakfast. I believe that the regular walking program we introduce is a substitute for what we take away. For the patients, it is a positive step toward taking charge of their own lives. They can discover the satisfaction of saying, "I'm in control. I'm doing this for my health." Not only will those people be healthier, they probably will realize there are other aspects of their lives they can change for the better. We know, for example, that people who exercise regularly are more careful about what they eat, less likely to smoke, and more likely to give up smoking cigarettes than people who do not exercise.

Working in cardiac rehabilitation, I witnessed the dramatic effect exercise had in restoring personal control, as well as facilitating physical recovery in patients with heart disease. Having seen that success, I set up the Exercise Physiology and Nutrition Laboratory in 1984. I wanted to take what we had learned from working with cardiac patients at the University of Massachusetts Medical Center, and see how it would work to prevent heart disease. My colleagues and I have since then researched a wide variety of projects and presented our findings in over thirty papers at major scientific and medical meetings, including the American College of Sports Medicine; the American Heart Association; the American Alliance for Health, Physical Education, Recreation and Dance; and the American Association of Cardiopulmonary Rehabilitation. An equally important goal of the laboratory is to explain to the public our findings concerning what people can do to make themselves healthier.

My partner in this endeavor is Ann Ward, Ph.D., the exercise physiologist who directs our laboratory and the co-author of this book. Ann first convinced me that a cardiologist and an exercise physiologist would make a good team in the effort to understand the impact of exercise on the heart. We added to our staff several postdoctoral fellows, a number of exercise physiologists, several research nurses, research assistants, and support staff. Recently we made a major commitment to nutrition research, a project led by Diane Morris, Ph.D. Our group has grown to be one of the largest exercise physiology and nutrition laboratories in the country, with a staff of twenty-five people.

Our projects are far-reaching. Currently we are studying the importance of hydration for performance; the role of walking for individuals who are on beta-blocker medications for hypertension; and the role of fiber cereal in lowering cholesterol. We are convinced that there are important discoveries to be made linking exercise and nutrition as elements in a positive lifestyle. We are also examining aspects of children's fitness.

We select projects that are potentially important for scientific understanding, but then we make the results public to help people make the changes they need to live longer and healthier lives.

I am always moved when I discover that our lab's information has enabled people to change their lives. Not long ago I was taking a plane to Denver. I sat down beside a young man who was reading *Fitness Walking,* a book I wrote with Rob Sweetgall. When I mentioned to him that I had worked on that project, he said, "Oh, my father gave me this," and showed me the inscription, "Ted, this is the book that saved my life." I felt very proud that the work we were doing had had such an impact on a person. For all fellow travelers on the road to fitness I hope the same benefits will come from reading *this* book.

JMR
Worcester, Massachusetts

ACKNOWLEDGMENTS

Research and writing are both collaborative efforts. We are deeply indebted to many individuals who have helped in the preparation of this book and the five years of walking research in our Exercise Physiology and Nutrition Laboratory which is summarized in it.

Through the years, we have been privileged to know a number of talented editors and writers. Two who made critical contributions to this book are Nancy Heffernan and Larry Rothstein.

Our professional colleagues have offered support, encouragement and helpful insights. Dr. Diane Morris, director of nutrition in our laboratory, generously contributed knowledge and editing skills for the nutrition chapter. Dr. Patty Freedson and Gayle Hutchinson made major contributions to the research on children's walking. Dr. Joseph Alpert, chief of the Division of Cardiovascular Medicine, and Dr. Ira Ockene, associate chief of the division, have been stalwart supporters of our research.

We are blessed with dedicated and talented assistants. Beth Porcaro, our editorial assistant, guides every step of the publication process for all of our major manuscripts, including this and other books. We simply could not do it without her efficiency and good humor. Jane Hodgkinson, Dr. Rippe's administrative assistant, and Mary Sosvielle, laboratory coordinator and Dr. Ward's administrative assistant, juggled the diverse demands of our careers and kept everything in order and moving forward.

Karen Eubanks, product development manager at EQUI-COR, has been a champion of this project from its inception. We are grateful to her. Roger Taylor, M.D., M.P.A., president of the Corporate HealthCare Management division of EQUI-COR and senior vice-president of EQUICOR assured both financial and technical support for the book. We are pleased to acknowledge the participation and help of EQUICOR, which made this book possible. As a premier employee benefits company, EQUICOR offers a full range of life, health, and disability insurance products and has a significant investment in keeping people healthy. The Corporate HealthCare Management division of EQUICOR, which offers health promotion and utilization management services, worked with us to create this book. In supporting this book, it was the goal of EQUICOR that it be a valuable resource to individuals in improving their health and quality of life.

Our friends at The Rockport Company have supported much of our walking research over the past five years. Bruce Katz, founder and former president of The Rockport Company, was an early supporter. Bob Infantino, senior vice-president for marketing and product development, Bob Meers, senior vice-president of sales, and Bob Slattery, president of The Rockport Company, have offered their continued support and encouragement. Reina Rago-O'Connor, former head of the Rockport Walking Institute℠ (RWI), and Robin Hillsamer, current director of the RWI, have helped in numerous ways. Carol Cone, president of Cone Communications, has been a constant and creative force behind our country's walking movement. A number of individuals at the McDonald's Corporation and the Ronald McDonald Children's Charities have made key contributions to our research in children's walking. Special thanks to Sandy Silver, Ken Barun, Mike Gordon, Chuck Rubner, and Bridget Marshall.

Our editor at Prentice Hall Press, Paul Aron, has pushed, prodded, and cajoled us through three book projects in the last eighteen months and never lost his enthusiasm or sense of humor. Brad Ketchum, editor of *The Walking Magazine,* has supplied us with excellent information, friendship, and insights.

Our staff of exercise physiologists, nutritionists, medical students, and graduate students both current and former have devoted time, energy, and talent to the research projects recounted in this book. While we cannot possibly list them all, some who made important contributions are: Lynn Ahlquist, Ph.D., Kathy Bell, M.S., Linda Botelho, M.S., R.D., Carmen Cononie, M.S., Paula Cuneo, R.D., Cara Ebbeling, M.S., Julie Fenster, M.S., Maureen Maher, B.S., Beverly McCraw, M.S., Stephanie O'Hanley, M.S., John Porcari, Ph.D., Carol Shustak, R.N., Don Sussman, Ph.D., Lauri Webber, M.S., and Merry Yamartino, R.D.

Finally, there are more than 1,000 volunteer research subjects, who have participated in walking research projects in our laboratory in the past five years. To all these individuals we are deeply grateful. Each of these people, in their own way, contributed to the goal of helping take charge of their lives by walking. While we accept responsibility for any errors or omissions in this book, the credit for the research that has helped us get America up on its feet and walking belongs to the thousands of people who have helped us along the way.

JAMES M. RIPPE, M.D.
ANN WARD, PH.D.
Worcester, Massachusetts

Dr. James M. Rippe's

COMPLETE
BOOK

OF

FITNESS
WALKING

1

WHY WALK?

Back in 1984, when we got involved in fitness walking, we had no idea how far-reaching the effects would be. We did not know how many thousands of people wanted to lead healthy lives, or how many would make fitness walking the cornerstone of their physical activity program.

Earlier, from 1981 to 1984, one of us had been the medical director of New England's largest cardiac rehabilitation program. Each year about six hundred patients were treated in this program who had suffered heart attacks, undergone bypass surgery, or were at high risk for heart disease. We put virtually every one of these patients on a regular program of walking, emphasizing the importance of healthy exercise in the recovery from heart attack. Equally important, we told them that walking allowed patients to play an active role in their own recovery. After suffering a tremendous psychological trauma, they had lost control of their bodies. Walking helped change that. By the end of 1984, we had several thousand patients on walking programs.

This kind of therapy is less than fifty years old. In fact, modern medicine itself is a relatively recent phenomenon. Doctors didn't know what a heart attack was until the early twentieth century. In the era before the Jazz Age they began to understand that the heart was the problem, but they still had no idea what caused attacks. Since doctors thought activity made the heart wear out, they often discouraged their patients from being active, typically prescribing rest for heart attack patients.

Dr. Paul Dudley White of Massachusetts General Hospital, the father of American cardiology and the founder of the American Heart Association in 1924, dramatically changed the treatment of heart attacks. In the early 1920s he began to say to his startled colleagues that they should encourage people to take a daily walk. He knew in his own life that walking made him feel better. Based on his own experience, he postulated that not only was a walk not dangerous, it was positively beneficial.

Not until the 1950s did his ideas start to change the way doctors handled people who had had heart attacks. Before that, the patient would spend six weeks in the hospital flat on his back so his heart could "heal." Doctors theorized that it took six weeks for a "scar" to form over the wound in the heart, and during that period the patient should do nothing strenuous. But Paul Dudley White and fellow cardiologist Samuel Levine at Boston's Peter Bent Brigham Hospital both began to dispute the bed-rest theory. They saw too many complications from this procedure: blood clots, pulmonary emboli (blood clots in the lungs), and urinary tract infections. Designed for activity, the human body cannot easily endure six weeks of lying in bed.

To get patients going, Levine invented the "Levine chair," an adjustable chair for cardiac patients to sit in after their heart attack as a prelude to getting them up and back on their feet. White, meanwhile, was encouraging his patients to get out of bed and begin a program of walking.

The pioneering approaches of White and Levine were paralleled by advances in medical knowledge. After World War II the scientific and medical communities were struggling not just to know how to treat patients who already had heart disease, they were also trying to understand why so many productive, young individuals died from heart disease. In 1946 the National Institutes of Health and other organizations began to support serious heart-disease research. A number of studies begun then have now borne fruit.

Chief among them is the Framingham Study started in the 1950s in the town of Framingham, Massachusetts. Researchers have studied a population of around 10,000 for more than thirty years and looked at factors that increase or decrease the risk of heart disease. In the 1950s researchers also looked at other large populations to find some of the conditions linked to heart disease. Evidence from these epidemiologic studies gradually began to reveal the role of activity in preventing heart disease.

In England, one of the early studies examined London bus drivers and conductors. Doctors discovered that conductors—who walked up and down the aisles and stairs of the double-decker buses collecting fares—had a markedly lower incidence of heart disease than did the bus drivers, who sat all day battling London traffic. In the United States, a study compared mail carriers, who made their rounds in rain, snow, and sleet, to postal clerks, who sat day after day and sorted letters. Here again, the incidence of heart disease among active mail carriers who walked daily was much lower than among sedentary postal clerks. Other studies compared active midwestern farmers to more sedentary factory workers. The results were the same. Some scientists criticized these projects, suggesting that the findings could have been the result of people selecting more active jobs because they were healthier. Whatever their faults, however, the results began to link health with physical activity.

In the 1970s Dr. Ralph Paffenbarger, professor at Stanford University in California and lecturer at the Harvard School of Public Health, and his colleagues compared shipping industry clerks with longshoremen who unloaded ships and were active year in and year out. Paffenbarger's careful methods ensured that neither group was intrinsically healthier than the other. The results confirmed earlier studies: People who were active at work had less heart disease than people who had sedentary jobs.

The question remained, however, whether leisure-time activities decreased the risk of heart disease. Paffenbarger studied 16,000 Harvard and University of Pennsylvania graduates who enrolled between 1916 and 1950. His "College Alumni Study" was published in the *New England Journal of Medicine* in 1986. It focused on the correlation between physical activity and length of life. Paffenbarger demonstrated that people who have been consistently active throughout their lives have significantly less likelihood of heart disease.

What does Paffenbarger mean by activity? He asked participants three questions about their activity: Do you walk five city blocks per day? Do you climb five flights of stairs a day? Do you engage in a half-hour of vigorous daily sports play? Paffenbarger found that the men who expended between 500 and 3,500 kilocalories a week in exercise (for purposes of the study one hour of vigorous activity was defined as equal to 500 kilocalories) were significantly less likely to suffer a heart attack than were their sedentary classmates. By age eighty those who exercised regularly could expect to add one or two years to their lives. Overall, the likelihood of heart attack decreased by 21 percent for men who walked nine miles a week. Besides supporting the other studies' conclusions concerning the benefits of physical activity, the landmark Paffenbarger study highlighted the value of the simple act of walking—up the stairs or on the street—as a way of increasing life expectancy.

In 1987, a major statistical study supported the idea that

vigorous exercise prevents heart disease. The Centers for Disease Control analyzed forty-three previous smaller studies of exercise that separated out risk factors other than inactivity. This study compared the risk of heart disease of the least active people in our society—about 60 percent of adult Americans fall into this least active group—with the most active people in our society. The study found that people who don't exercise on a regular basis have twice the risk of developing heart disease as those who do. Put in another perspective, being inactive increases the risk of heart disease as much as smoking a pack of cigarettes a day. The difference is that only 10 percent of people in our society smoke a pack of cigarettes a day, whereas 60 percent are inactive.

Since World War II more than forty increasingly accurate scientific studies of every imaginable group—from Masai herdsmen in Africa to Finnish lumberjacks—have agreed that physical activity carried on consistently throughout a lifetime improves health. For Western cultures this could translate into a marked decrease in heart disease. Those studies uniformly suggest that the most important aspect of exercise is not how intensely a person exercises—in the Paffenbarger study intensity was not even a question—but that he or she exercise *consistently.* That is where walking fits in so beautifully. Walking is something you can do consistently and easily throughout your life.

The Beginning of Fitness Walking

A national-parks survey in 1983 indicated that 55 million people in North America were walking as a form of exercise. In 1985 alone another 8 million people adopted walking as their primary fitness activity, making it the fastest-growing participant sport on the continent, according to a survey conducted by the National Sporting Goods Manufacturing Association.

Why has walking become such a popular activity? First of all, people have been bombarded with information telling them to be active in order to lose weight, look better, be healthier, and live longer. From the TV ads for Special K to dire warnings from the American Heart Association and the Surgeon General, baby boomers have learned that exercise is important. And it's our experience that the average person really wants to do the right things where health is concerned.

Part of this tremendous response, however, has to do with the substantial evidence that walking is just about the perfect exercise. Most of this knowledge is new and largely from our lab. In 1984, The Rockport Company, a leading manufacturer of walking shoes whose headquarters were located in the town next to the University of Massachusetts Medical School, asked if we would do research to find out if walking was a beneficial activity for the average person. Specifically, Rockport wanted us to study a man who was planning a monumental walk to all fifty states to bring a simple message to America's children: Get some daily exercise, pay attention to what you eat, and don't smoke. The purpose of the walk was to dramatize to children that if you did those three things, the risk of heart disease would be greatly reduced.

We were intrigued. This spectacular feat—if it could be pulled off—would deliver a message to children very similar to what physicians tell adult heart patients. And it was a message long overdue. By the time children reach the age of twelve in our society, 40 percent of them have at least one major risk factor of heart disease. Studies have shown clearly that there are signs of heart disease that develop in childhood. It was an important message for the American public.

When the walk started out in September of 1984, a team of scientists was assembled to follow our subject's progress for a year. The solo walk was accomplished through all fifty states. (Of course, with flights to Alaska and Hawaii.) Six times during the year our walker stopped his walk and was picked up by a car, driven to the nearest airport, and flown to the exercise physiology laboratory at the medical center for thirty-six hours of intensive testing. The tests generated more than one million pieces of data, the largest single study of one human being ever undertaken.

Our subject would fly back to the state that he had left, be driven to the exact spot on the road where he had been picked up, and resume his walk. When he finished, he had covered 11,208 miles in 363 days, averaging 1.25 marathons a day for an entire year. The message from the walk reached more than 100,000 children and was delivered to audiences in schools and community meetings all across the nation. All major national television networks and every major national publication highlighted his walk.

This walk and the scientific studies we did in conjunction with it were the start of the modern walking movement, because we tapped into something extremely powerful. The walk energized people around the country who were already walkers or who felt that the fitness movement had passed them by. They wanted to do something for themselves, to take charge of their lives, and to feel healthy on a daily basis.

Though we had collected a lot of interesting data during this incredible walk (our subject consumed 20 percent more oxygen than the average male of his age, height, and weight; he lost fat but not lean muscle during his walk; and the efficiency of his stride improved over the course of his walk), average people couldn't relate his accomplishment to themselves. He had condensed a lifetime of walking into one year. Most people cannot walk the thirty-three miles a day that he averaged, and certainly the average person is not going to walk 11,208 miles in one year. So, as we continued our scientific study of the effects of fitness walking on this extraordinary man, we began investigating the effects of the normal distances and paces that an average person would walk.

Our findings were tremendously exciting. For example, we studied a group of women aged twenty to seventy-nine and found that if a woman increased her walking speed from three to four miles per hour, more than 90 percent of them elevated their heart rate into what we call the "target training zone," the heart-rate zone in which one achieves optimal cardiovascular benefits. We discovered similar dramatic results among men who engaged in one mile of fitness walking. Two-thirds of men aged twenty to seventy-nine got their heart rate into the target training zone by walking at the rate of four miles per hour. Eighty-three percent of men over age fifty got their heart rate up into the target training zone simply by walking at a slightly brisker pace than average for a mile. It became obvious to us that the vast majority of Americans could get into better shape just by walking.

As we began releasing our findings to the public, people started learning what fitness walking could do for them. Ours and other medical reports have concluded that walking will produce similar results in short-term training and in long-term health benefits as any other aerobic sport.

With the rise of the walking movement, for the first time a huge number of people are taking control of their health. A great many of those people are baby boomers who are now in their late thirties and early forties. They are seeking a program supported by the medical literature, but they won't stay with a program that is uncomfortable. They're looking for an exercise that makes common sense. We like to call it a "populist sport"—a sport which is truly for the majority of people. It doesn't require elaborate facilities. It's social. It's the kind of activity a person can engage in with his or her family. It can be done almost anywhere and any time by anyone regardless of age, sex, or physical condition. It is the exercise for the individual who understands that consistency is important—that one day leads to another and that one's actions carry consequences, but that you don't achieve everything in life in one day.

The Historical Perspective

The recent popularity of fitness walking is only the latest development in what has long been regarded as a beneficial activity. Virtually every advanced culture has understood that a sound mind and a sound body somehow relate to each other. According to an old Hindu proverb, "Walking makes for a long life." Certainly the Greeks, who began the Olympic Games, believed in physical fitness. The Roman orator Cicero proclaimed that daily activity was one of the ways a man could carry some of his youthful vigor into his later years. The English have always believed in the healthful benefits of walking. In the eighteenth century in England people created mazes and gardens for walking. Dr. Samuel Johnson, the famous lexicographer and essayist, was noted for his perambulations around London. The poet William Wordsworth and his sister Dorothy, as well as many other young men and women of the period, took walking tours of Europe.

In the United States walking became a popular sport around the turn of the century with the advent of six-day races, one of the fiercest competitive events of the time. The most popular of the walking champions was Edward Payson Weston, a newspaperman from Providence, Rhode Island. People all along the route cheered Weston, who regularly covered well over four hundred miles in those competitions while wearing a tie and a bowler hat. In 1904, when he was seventy-one years old, he walked from San Francisco to New York City in 104 days, averaging more than forty miles a day. By the time Weston died at age ninety-one, the "evening constitutional" was part of American life.

Since Weston's epic walks, four United States presidents have focused the nation's attention on walking.

At the turn of the century, President Theodore Roosevelt was famed as a walker. Roosevelt had suffered from asthma and other health problems as a child and had conquered them largely through vigorous exercise. In 1909, the year he left the presidency, he demonstrated his fitness by walking fifty miles in three days.

Forty years later President Harry Truman reinstated the evening constitutional as an institution. He set a brisk pace that he described as "walking as though I have someplace to go," which we like to think is our first definition of fitness walking. He went at a clip that left his less fit Secret Service bodyguards and any White House reporters who tried to follow panting after him.

When President Dwight Eisenhower suffered a heart attack in 1955 and Dr. Paul Dudley White was called in to treat him, the revolution in modern cardiac rehabilitation went public. The nation was fearful that the sixty-five-year-old president would not survive a second term. White went on television to reassure the country that if Eisenhower adopted a program of walking (among other things) he could resume his duties as president. White's announcement calmed fears while explaining to people that heart-attack patients should not retire and lead a sedentary life.

In 1963 President Kennedy created a nationwide walking craze when he speculated about whether the Marine Corps could repeat Theodore Roosevelt's fifty-mile walk. U.S. Marine Commandant David M. Shoup accepted the challenge for the Corps and issued marching orders to marines everywhere. Then civilians across the country answered the call—children, men, women, students, Boy Scouts, veteran walkers. All set out to prove they could repeat Roosevelt's accomplishment. At Camp Lejeune, North Carolina, Second Lt. Martin Shimek, a former marathoner, set the military record by walking fifty miles in nine hours and fifty-three minutes wearing a twenty-five-pound pack, a ten-pound helmet, and a pistol that slapped against his hip at every step. Robert Kennedy and his dog finished the fifty miles, as did many others. For a time hundreds of people became infected with the so-called "fifty-mile madness."

Public perception lagged behind scientific knowledge

and even presidential challenges, however. Since the public could not yet believe that walking was an excellent exercise for preventing heart disease, in the late sixties and seventies running and aerobic dance rather than walking became the most popular exercises for fitness. Through these exercises a whole generation of people came to understand how good it feels to be physically fit. In fact, the postwar baby boomers found jogging or running such a satisfactory exercise that they sometimes viewed running as a panacea and a kind of religious experience. We probably all remember being lectured by friends who tried to convince us of jogging's greatness. But increasingly we have become aware of the drawbacks of running, jogging, and aerobics.

When people jog, they land with three or four times their body weight. Every time they leap up in the air in aerobic dance they land with four or five times their body weight. As runners and aerobic dancers enter their forties, they still want to remain physically fit, but they increasingly experience knee, back, or ankle injuries. In walking, by definition, you always have one foot on the ground. You land with only one to one and a half times your weight. We believe there are fewer injuries associated with walking than with jogging or aerobic dance. Certainly it is less painful to the joints and bones.

The tragic death of runner Jim Fixx in the summer of 1984 underscored what we had been discovering scientifically. Fixx, regarded as the guru of the running movement, died while running on a back road in Vermont. People in this country were shocked, and many began to rethink their exercise habits.

Many people drew the mistaken conclusion that exercise is dangerous. Before Fixx discovered running, however, he had been significantly overweight, he had had extremely high cholesterol levels for many years, early in his life he had smoked heavily, and he had had a family history of serious heart disease—all major risk factors for a heart attack. Running did not cause Fixx's death, but his death did lead people to understand that running is not the only path to a healthy life.

Once people realized that running is not magic and that exercise doesn't have to be painful, they started dancing, weight training, and walking. They stopped smoking and controlled cholesterol by careful eating and drinking. This is a much more realistic approach to health and exercise than running by itself.

The Physical Benefits of Walking

Retirement from his teaching job left Ted depressed and at loose ends. For months he sat in front of the television set, ate snacks, drank beer, and watched his weight mushroom. Concerned about Ted's weight and his blood pressure, his family doctor advised him to exercise and lose a substantial amount of weight. A year later Ted credits his adherence to his fitness-walking program with turning his life around. The trim, happy Ted has his blood pressure under control and as an added bonus has learned to love walking.

Looking back on her years of inactivity and poor eating habits, Allison, aged thirty-five, observed, "I was walking through a minefield and I didn't even know it. I ate all the wrong things, put on a lot of weight, and never took any exercise. I hated being overweight, but when I learned what my cholesterol was, I was shocked." After three years of fitness walking and watching her diet, Allison's cholesterol is under control, her cardiovascular system is much more efficient, she has lost twenty-two pounds, and her self-esteem has risen. When she was told she looked ten years younger, she laughed. "I'm expecting to live ten years longer."

Walking strengthens the heart and improves its performance. In the laboratory we measure the efficiency of a person's heart through maximum exercise tolerance tests in which a person walks on a treadmill at increasing speeds up increasingly steeper angles. If an individual exercises to his maximum capacity until he cannot continue, we can measure the maximum ability of his heart to pump out blood (the cardiac output) plus the maximum ability of his exercising muscles to extract oxygen out of the blood. These two factors combined tell us his maximum oxygen consumption, which is expressed as the term *max VO2*. That is the body's highest total aerobic exercise capacity. If a person has been physically inactive and begins a regular fitness-walking program, his exercise capacity increases significantly after eight to twelve weeks. By the end of that time he will be able to walk farther, faster, and at a steeper incline. Fitness walking is one of the very best ways of improving the max VO2 because it helps the strength and efficiency of your heart and muscles.

Apart from these health benefits, fitness walking is also one of the best ways of improving cardiac health and reducing the chances of a heart attack. As we know from studies by Dr. Paffenbarger and others, a long-term daily program of walking significantly reduces the likelihood of developing coronary artery disease.

In fact, a fitness-walking program consistently improves almost every system of the body and makes a major contribution to the quality and duration of a person's life. Here is a thumbnail sketch of the improvements in health that you can expect from a regular walking program:

Losing weight: With 20 percent of Americans seriously obese, weight control is a major public health issue. Walking is so crucial to every diet plan that we will spend a whole chapter discussing this problem. For now, consider that walking briskly over the course of a year for forty-five minutes a day, four times a week, burns eighteen pounds of fat if food consumption remains stable.

Lowering cholesterol: In the late 1980s the American Heart Association and the Surgeon General released reports on the danger that Americans face from high cholesterol. A recent study of postmen who walk many miles per day showed that they had higher levels of high-density lipoproteins, which are useful in lowering the levels of cholesterol.

Reducing conditions associated with hypertension: Though no one knows exactly what causes high blood pressure, walking improves two conditions often associated with it—stress and obesity.

Slowing aging and the decline in aerobic capacity: While aerobic capacity diminishes with age, the rate of decline is probably often the result of long-term inactivity rather than simply aging.

Increasing strength, flexibility, and balance: As people get older, their level of fitness becomes an important factor in their ability to climb stairs, get in and out of the bath, and perform other daily tasks that allow them to remain independent. One good way to increase strength, flexibility, and balance is through a program of physical fitness.

Strengthening bones: While the shape and size of bones are determined largely by genetic factors, the density of bones is controlled mainly by diet, hormones, and exercise. As people get older, bones become thinner and more brittle. Fortunately, bones, like muscles, become stronger with use in such impact exercises as running or walking.

Aiding diabetics: Because walking decreases the need for insulin, helps control weight (a major problem for diabetics), and lowers the risk of cardiovascular disease (the number one killer of diabetics), many doctors prescribe walking to their patients with diabetes.

Increasing stamina: Exercise increases a person's energy and ability to work and play longer and harder without fatigue.

The Mental Benefits of Walking

The physical benefits of fitness walking are cumulative. They accrue from exercise on a regular basis, and they depend on a consistent program of fitness walking. On the other hand, the mental health rewards can be collected from the very first walk.

Almost every walker reports that his mental attitude improves when he or she starts to walk. Spirits are lifted as depression and anxiety are diminished. The National Institute of Mental Health indicates that long-term exercise decreases depression in moderately depressed patients, and increases self-esteem in normal people. Executives frequently report that regular exercise lowers their sense of stress.

According to a 1983 survey in *The Physician and Sportsmedicine,* more than 90 percent of doctors prescribe exercise to help people control depression and anxiety. We ran extensive tests in our laboratory to see if this prescription was worthwhile. We had thirty-six volunteers take a psychological test to determine their degree of anxiety and tension and then walk on a treadmill for forty minutes at slow, medium, fast, and self-selected speeds. After the walk we tested them again and discovered they were significantly less anxious and tense, regardless of the speed at which they had walked. Levels of anxiety remained lower for about two hours. Other research indicates that anxiety is decreased for much longer—perhaps up to four hours—if walking is strenuous.

To be sure that walking alone caused the mood change, we specifically took away some of the things that people normally find most pleasurable about walking, like talking to other people and being out in the sun. In addition, all of the investigators wore white lab coats and read the volunteers a standard statement before they went on the treadmill saying, "We will not be talking to you during the time that you are on the treadmill. Not because we are not interested, but because we don't want any extraneous conversation to in any way change how you might be feeling."

Besides lowering levels of anxiety and tension, walking gives people a tremendous sense of well-being. We call this a "walker's high." Walkers' bodies seem to go into overdrive. One woman, aged forty-seven, described it thus: "I reach a point that I call cruise. It happens every time . . . I thought it only happened to runners. My legs are just going and my mind is off to Bermuda or wherever."

Just what causes this high is not clear. One theory is that body chemicals called endorphins, which cause a sense of well-being, increase during physical activity. Some scientists think a slight rise in body temperature may contribute to the sense of well-being.

Others feel it may have less to do with raising body temperature than it does with doing rhythmic exercise. Long-time joggers or swimmers also experience this sense of inner peace. The walker establishes a relationship with some inner rhythm in his body. We call this phenomenon *entrainment*. All this is speculation, but we know, for example, that horses breathe in regular patterns that change when they walk, trot, or gallop. When a person gets involved in a rhythmic exercise like walking, it touches deeper, currently unexplained rhythms in the body and that connection frees the mind in some way.

Wherever these mental experiences come from, people shouldn't ignore them. Ask yourself, How do I feel? Do I feel calmer? Do I feel better? Am I thinking clearer? You'll identify these mental benefits, and that will provide an incentive to continue walking.

Recently researchers have become interested in the relationship of posture and mood. According to one study, people who walk with a long stride, with arms swinging, are reflecting independence, friendliness, and confidence, while shufflers tend to be meeker and less friendly. If a person's walk is rigid and uptight, it probably reflects how he is thinking. The good news is that if he improves his walking posture, if he lifts his head, frees his gait, and straightens his shoulders, his attitude will improve. If he looks confident, friendly, and relaxed, he will actually feel the way he looks.

As people continue to walk and become more physically fit, the list of mental benefits grows. Walkers report improved self-confidence and self-esteem, as well as increased concentration and efficiency in mental activities.

Living Longer by Fitness Walking

There is no doubt that people who are physically active on a regular basis feel better physically and mentally than people who are not. That alone is enough to recommend walking to every adult in America. And, as we have seen, the College Alumni Study established that regular walking also extends the length of life.

One of our colleagues said recently, "If I were a drug manufacturer, and I found a drug that would make you feel better every day you took it; and if you took it every day throughout your life, your life would be two years longer, I would be a multimillionaire for having made that discovery." Well, there is such a drug. It's called walking.

A huge number of people are taking that prescription. What has happened in the last five years has been phenomenal. *The Walking Magazine* now has a circulation of over 700,000. A tremendous interest in fitness walking was waiting to be tapped because, we like to think, fitness walking is intuitively correct. Our grandfathers and grandmothers and great-grandfathers and great-grandmothers intuitively knew that the "evening constitutional" was a good idea. Now, a hundred years after all the technology and all the fads have come and gone, we have come back to something that we knew all along—it's good for your health to go out and take a walk.

2

GETTING STARTED

Perhaps during a routine physical examination your doctor tells you your blood pressure is too high and recommends that you begin regular exercise. Or you realize that much as you enjoy a day of sightseeing, you find it exhausting. Or you look in the mirror after your morning shower and are more annoyed than ever by those extra pounds. Or the last time you went running, your knee began to give you trouble again. You've read that fitness walking is the best exercise program around. You're convinced, and you decide that you want to begin walking.

When you have arrived at this crucial decision, the temptation is to demand improvement overnight, which is impossible. Aerobic fitness only increases between 1 and 3 percent a week. If, after being sedentary for years, you begin in a burst of enthusiasm and walk four miles a day for three days, you will get sore, tired, and discouraged, and will risk injuring yourself. On the other hand, if you begin with too easy a program, you won't get optimal benefits, and you may become discouraged because you aren't progressing. Setting *realistic goals* is the first key to a successful fitness-walking program.

To set such goals you need to know your current fitness level. Then you can begin with a program that fits your initial physical state and increases in length and speed as your strength and aerobic capacity improve. Knowing your level of fitness also gives you a benchmark against which to gauge your progress.

A simple and reliable walking fitness test you could perform at home did not exist until recently. In the early 1920s the Harvard Fatigue Laboratory constructed a test in which a person dragged a sled weighted with stones for 300 yards and then had his heart rate measured. That test proved impractical because it took too much space and required too much equipment. The same lab then developed the Harvard Step Test in which people stepped up and down from a bench for five minutes. This was the test that many World War II recruits did as part of their army physical. The problem with that test was that the subject's quadriceps (the large muscle in the front of the thighs) would often fatigue before he could do enough exercise to accurately test his cardiovascular fitness. Various labs developed other tests—riding a stationary bicycle, or running for twelve minutes, or running for a mile and a half. Since the stationary cycle test involved special equipment and the running tests proved impossible, dangerous, or at least uncomfortable for some people, the usefulness of these tests was limited.

Until 1986 no scientifically validated and convenient "field" test (a "field" test is one that you can do outside of a laboratory setting) of aerobic capacity used walking to test fitness. The only reasonably accurate tests required high-tech equipment and cost high-tech prices.

At the University of Massachusetts Exercise Physiology and Nutrition Laboratory, we set out to address that problem. Sponsored by The Rockport Walking Institute, we tested 343 men and women for eighteen months under very rigorous circumstances. We made direct measurements of their maximal oxygen consumption—their max VO2—and had them walk a mile, or four laps of a quarter-mile track. We correlated the two measures. At first we tested people twice because we thought they might not understand how to pace themselves around the track. We assumed we would get quite different results the second time they walked the mile. We soon discovered that in more than 90 percent of the cases, people immediately figured out the correct pace for walking briskly for a mile.

As long as one foot is kept on the ground, the test works for anybody and any kind of walking. (Running is not allowed.) How fit a person is makes no difference. The test works for a swimmer or a tennis player or a sedentary person.

There are a few limitations to taking this test. A serious orthopedic problem or an injury that makes it difficult for you to walk renders the test impossible. Consult your doctor if you have been inactive and are over forty-five, or if you have any question as to whether the test is safe for you. *The test is not for people on beta-blocker medication for heart disease or high blood pressure.* (We are hard at work, however, at developing a test that is accurate for such people.)

What, then, is the Rockport Fitness Walking Test (RFWT)? It is a measure of how well your heart, lungs, and blood vessels work to deliver oxygen-rich blood to the muscles and how efficiently the muscles utilize the oxygen. It can be done by people at any level of fitness, and between the ages of twenty and seventy-nine years old. It can be done without professional assistance or special equipment.

We first reported the test in 1986 at the American College of Sports Medicine and subsequently on *Good Morning America* and the *Today Show.* Major newspapers provided extensive coverage. In the last two years, more than a million people have requested information about the RFWT.

To do the RFWT all you need to know are your age, sex,

the time it takes you to walk the mile, and your heart rate immediately after walking a mile. After that you use the charts developed from the tests we did on our volunteers. The RFWT shows if your fitness level is high, above average, average, below average, or low for age groups twenty to twenty-nine, thirty to thirty-nine, forty to forty-nine, fifty to fifty-nine, sixty or higher.

Before you begin, you need to learn to take your pulse. For that you need a watch with a second hand. And you will need to practice a few times. Here's how:

While sitting still, place your first and second fingers (not your thumb) gently on your wrist, or on the side of your neck. On your wrist you will feel the pulse in the radial artery, which is just inside the wrist bone on the thumb side. In your neck the pulse is just below the angle of the jawbone at the level of the Adam's apple. Press gently, otherwise you can get an inaccurate reading.

Count your pulse for fifteen seconds and multiply by four to get your heart rate per minute. That gives you your *resting heart rate*. At the end of the test you are going to take your *exercise heart rate*.

Once you can take your pulse with confidence, you are ready to take the RFWT. First you need to find a place to take the test. A track is best, since a mile is already measured and you won't be interrupted by car traffic. Health clubs and your local high school normally have quarter-mile tracks you can use. Another alternative is to use your car's odometer to measure out a one-mile course on a flat road with no stop signs or stop lights.

Wear comfortable loose-fitting clothes and a pair of well-designed walking shoes. As with any exercise, stretch and then walk slowly for two or three minutes to build up your pace, warm up, and accelerate your heart rate before beginning the test.

Now you are ready. Walk the mile as briskly as possible, trying to maintain as even a pace as you can. When you have finished, note the time in minutes and seconds; then *immediately* take your pulse, since your heart rate slows down rapidly after you stop walking. Count the beats for fifteen seconds and multiply by four to get the number of beats per minute. At the end of the test a person's heart rate is typically twenty-five to forty beats in fifteen seconds. When you multiply that by four you will know your exercise heart rate. Remember your results.

Here's an example of how it works. On the Rockport Fitness Walking Test a fifty-two-year-old woman walks a mile in seventeen minutes and fifteen seconds and her heart rate is 132 beats per minute at the end of the mile. On the Relative Fitness Chart for women fifty to fifty-nine years old, she finds seventeen minutes and fifteen seconds on the horizontal line (the time line) and draws a vertical line to the point where it

FIGURE 1

Example of Relative Fitness Chart for 50- to 59-Year-Old Woman

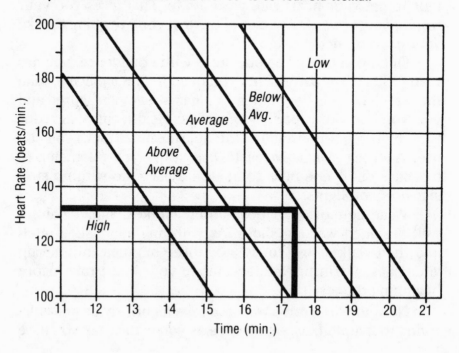

meets a horizontal line drawn through 132 on the heart rate line. The point where those two lines intersect on the Relative Fitness Chart is within the average range for fifty- to fifty-nine-year-old women (Figure 1).

On the Exercise Program Chart for women fifty to fifty-nine years old (Figure 2), again use her heart rate and time results to locate the program designed for her level of fitness, which is called Green. The next day she begins her ideal fitness-walking program (Figure 3). During the first two weeks of the Green program, she follows the routine listed under Week 1–2. She warms up for five to seven minutes and walks one and a half miles at three miles per hour. She should get her heart rate up to 60 to 70 percent of her maximum heart rate, or about 100 beats per minute. After her walk, she cools down and stretches for five to seven minutes. She follows this routine for five days per week. At the end of the second week, she moves into the second phase of the Green program; after the fourth week, the next phase; and so on. When she has finished the twenty-week program, she should retest herself with the RFWT to establish her new program.

To do the same for yourself, take your results from the Rockport Fitness Walking Test. Find your fitness level on the Relative Fitness Chart for your age and sex (Figure 4). Next find your exercise program among the Exercise Program graphs for your age and sex (Figure 4). Follow the color-coded twenty-week exercise program that corresponds with the Exercise Program graph (Figure 5).

This test is your instrument panel as you begin your fitness-walking program. It tells you how far and how fast to go. As you follow the program, it also informs you how far you have come. Watching your progress is good for motivation.

To understand how the fitness walking programs work, you have to grasp the concept of *target heart rate zone,* or *target training zone.* An individual gets the optimal benefit

FIGURE 2

Example of Exercise Program Chart for 50- to 59-Year-Old Woman

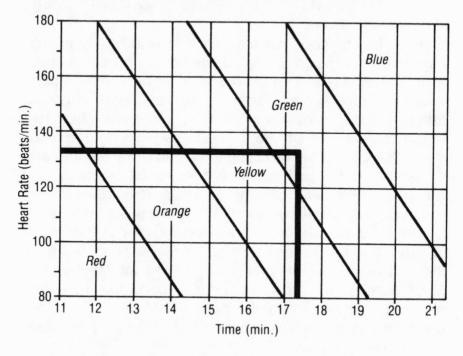

from aerobic training when the exercise activity maintains heart rate between a certain minimum number of beats per minute (the target training zone). The zone is from 60 to 80 percent of *predicted maximum heart rate.* To determine the predicted maximum heart rate and the target training zone, first subtract your age in years from 220. Next find your target training zone by multiplying your predicted maximum heart rate first by 0.6, then by 0.8. Figure 6 shows the target training zones.

For example, a man who is forty-five years old would subtract 45 from 220 and get 175. That is his predicted maximum heart rate. Then he would multiply 175 by 0.6 and get 105. That is the lower end of the target training zone. Then he would multiply 175 by 0.8 and get 140. That is the

FIGURE 3

GREEN PROGRAM

Week	1-2	3-4	5-6	7	8-9	10-12	13	14	15-16	17-18	19-20
WARM-UP (mins. before walk stretches)	5-7	5-7	5-7	5-7	5-7	5-7	5-7	5-7	5-7	5-7	5-7
MILEAGE	1.5	1.75	2.0	2.0	2.25	2.5	2.75	2.75	3.0	3.25	3.5
PACE (mph)	3.0	3.0	3.0	3.5	3.5	3.5	3.5	4.0	4.0	4.0	4.0
HEART RATE (% of max)	60-70	60-70	60-70	70	70	70	70	70-80	70-80	70-80	70-80
COOL-DOWN (mins. after walk stretches)	5-7	5-7	5-7	5-7	5-7	5-7	5-7	5-7	5-7	5-7	5-7
FREQUENCY (times per week)	5	5	5	5	5	5	5	5	5	5	5

*At the end of the twenty-week fitness-walking protocol, retest yourself to establish your new program.

FIGURE 4

Relative Fitness Levels and Exercise Programs for the Rockport Fitness Walking Test

20–29-Year-Old Males
Relative Fitness Level

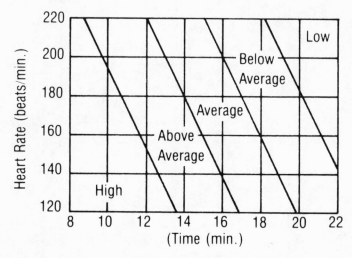

20–29-Year-Old Males
Exercise Program

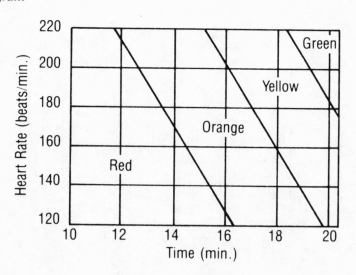

**20–29-Year-Old Females
Relative Fitness Level**

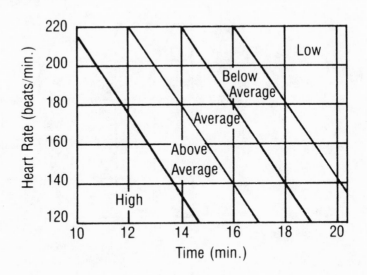

**20–29-Year-Old Females
Exercise Program**

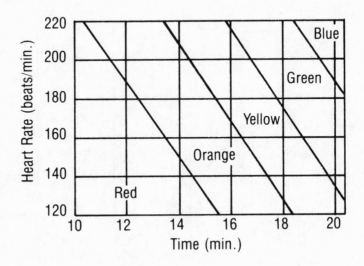

**30–39-Year-Old Males
Relative Fitness Level**

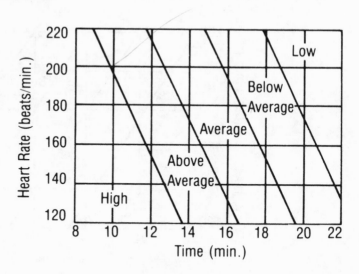

**30–39-Year-Old Males
Exercise Program**

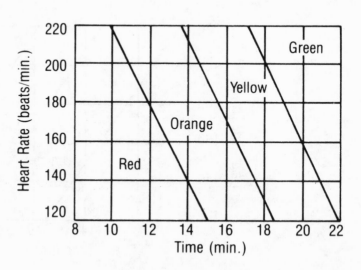

30–39-Year-Old Females
Relative Fitness Level

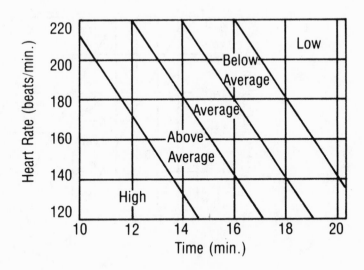

30–39-Year-Old Females
Exercise Program

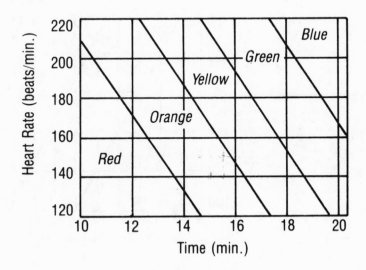

**40–49-Year-Old Males
Relative Fitness Level**

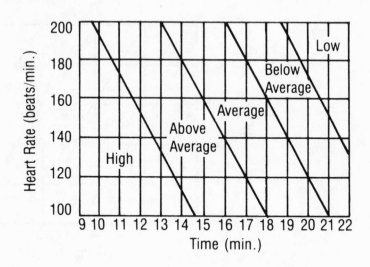

**40–49-Year-Old Males
Exercise Program**

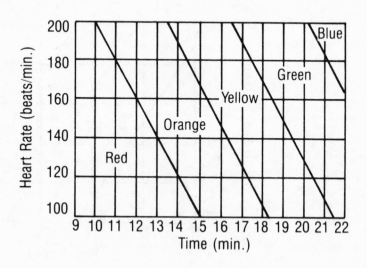

**40–49-Year-Old Females
Relative Fitness Level**

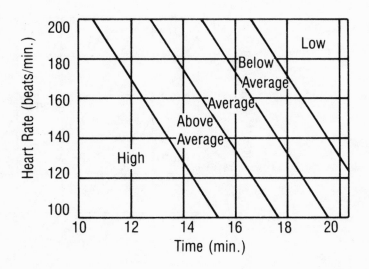

**40–49-Year-Old Females
Exercise Program**

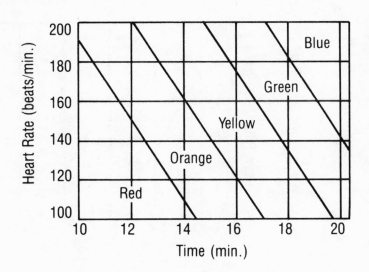

**50–59-Year-Old Males
Relative Fitness Level**

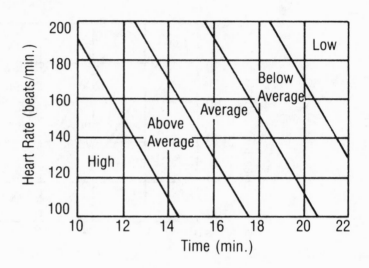

**50–59-Year-Old Males
Exercise Program**

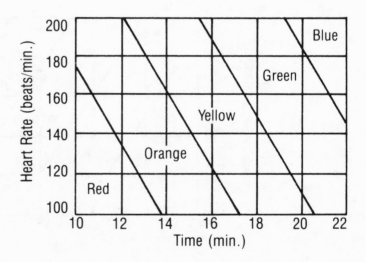

**50–59-Year-Old Females
Relative Fitness Level**

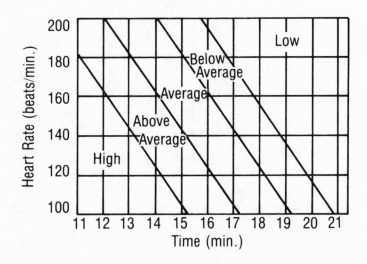

**50–59-Year-Old Females
Exercise Program**

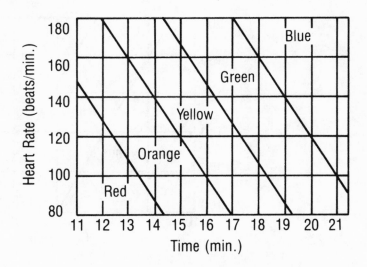

**60 + Year-Old Males
Relative Fitness Level**

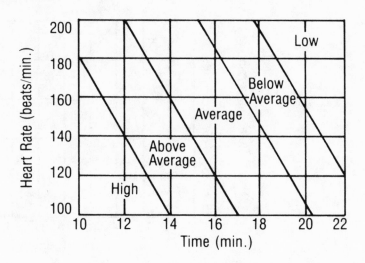

**60 + Year-Old Males
Exercise Program**

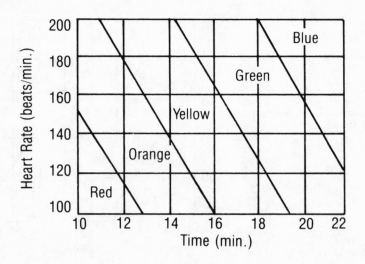

60 + Year-Old Females
Relative Fitness Level

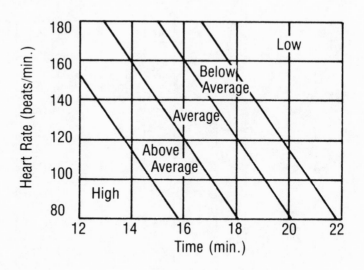

60 + Year-Old Females
Exercise Program

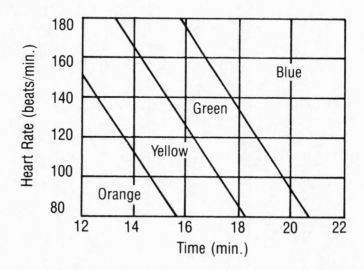

FIGURE 5
Fitness Walking Programs

BLUE PROGRAM*

Week	1-2	3-4	5	6	7-8	9	10	11	12-13	14	15-16	17-18	19-20
WARM-UP (mins. before walk stretches)	5-7	5-7	5-7	5-7	5-7	5-7	5-7	5-7	5-7	5-7	5-7	5-7	5-7
MILEAGE	1.0	1.25	1.5	1.5	1.75	2.0	2.0	2.0	2.25	2.5	2.5	2.75	3.0
PACE (mph)	3.0	3.0	3.0	3.5	3.5	3.5	3.75	3.75	3.75	3.75	4.0	4.0	4.0
HEART RATE (% of max)	60	60	60	60-70	60-70	60-70	60-70	70	70	70	70	70-80	70-80
COOL-DOWN (mins. after walk stretches)	5-7	5-7	5-7	5-7	5-7	5-7	5-7	5-7	5-7	5-7	5-7	5-7	5-7
FREQUENCY (times per week)	5	5	5	5	5	5	5	5	5	5	5	5	5

*At the end of the twenty-week fitness-walking protocol, retest yourself to establish your new program.

GREEN PROGRAM*

Week	1-2	3-4	5-6	7	8-9	10-12	13	14	15-16	17-18	19-20
WARM-UP (mins. before walk stretches)	5-7	5-7	5-7	5-7	5-7	5-7	5-7	5-7	5-7	5-7	5-7
MILEAGE	1.5	1.75	2.0	2.0	2.25	2.5	2.75	2.75	3.0	3.25	3.5
PACE (mph)	3.0	3.0	3.0	3.5	3.5	3.5	3.5	4.0	4.0	4.0	4.0
HEART RATE (% of max)	60-70	60-70	60-70	70	70	70	70	70-80	70-80	70-80	70-80
COOL-DOWN (mins. after walk stretches)	5-7	5-7	5-7	5-7	5-7	5-7	5-7	5-7	5-7	5-7	5-7
FREQUENCY (times per week)	5	5	5	5	5	5	5	5	5	5	5

*At the end of the twenty-week fitness-walking protocol, retest yourself to establish your new program.

YELLOW PROGRAM*

Week	1	2	3–4	5	6–8	9–10	11–12	13–14	15	16–17	18–20
WARM-UP (mins. before walk stretches)	5–7	5–7	5–7	5–7	5–7	5–7	5–7	5–7	5–7	5–7	5–7
MILEAGE	2.0	2.25	2.5	2.75	2.75	3.0	3.0	3.25	3.5	3.5	4.0
PACE (mph)	3.0	3.0	3.0	3.0	3.5	3.5	4.0	4.0	4.0	4.5	4.5
HEART RATE (% of max)	70	70	70	70	70	70	70–80	70–80	70–80	70–80	70–80
COOL-DOWN (mins. after walk stretches)	5–7	5–7	5–7	5–7	5–7	5–7	5–7	5–7	5–7	5–7	5–7
FREQUENCY (times per week)	5	5	5	5	5	5	5	5	5	5	5

*At the end of the twenty-week fitness-walking protocol, you may either retest yourself and move to a new fitness-walking category or follow the Yellow Maintenance Program for a lifetime of fitness walking.

38

ORANGE PROGRAM*

Week	1	2	3–4	5	6	7	8	9–10	11–14	15–20
WARM-UP (mins. before walk stretches)	5–7	5–7	5–7	5–7	5–7	5–7	5–7	5–7	5–7	5–7
MILEAGE	2.5	2.75	3.0	3.25	3.25	3.5	3.75	4.0	4.0	4.0
PACE (mph)	3.5	3.5	3.5	3.5	4.0	4.0	4.0	4.0	4.5	4.5
~~INCLINE/WEIGHT~~ Time (min)	43	47	51	56	49	53	56	60	53	+**
HEART RATE (% of max)	70	70	70	70	70–80	70–80	70–80	70–80	70–80	70–80
COOL-DOWN (mins. after walk stretches)	5–7	5–7	5–7	5–7	5–7	5–7	5–7	5–7	5–7	5–7
FREQUENCY (times per week)	5	5	5	5	5	5	5	5	5	3

*At the end of the twenty-week fitness-walking protocol, follow the Orange/Red Maintenance Program for a lifetime of fitness walking.
**During weeks 15–20, arm weights or incline may be added to increase intensity.

RED PROGRAM*

Week	1	2	3	4	5	6	7-20
WARM-UP (mins. before walk stretches)	5-7	5-7	5-7	5-7	5-7	5-7	5-7
MILEAGE	3.0	3.25	3.5	3.5	3.75	4.0	4.0
PACE (mph)	4.0	4.0	4.0	4.5	4.5	4.5	4.5
INCLINE/WEIGHT							+**
HEART RATE (% of max)	70	70	70	70-80	70-80	70-80	70-80
COOL-DOWN (mins. after walk stretches)	5-7	5-7	5-7	5-7	5-7	5-7	5-7
FREQUENCY (times per week)	5	5	5	5	5	5	3

*At the end of the twenty-week fitness-walking protocol, turn to the Orange/Red Maintenance Program for a lifetime of fitness walking.
**During weeks 15-20, arm weights or incline may be added to increase intensity.

YELLOW MAINTENANCE PROGRAM

WARM-UP: 5–7 minutes before walk stretches

AEROBIC WORK OUT: mileage: 4.0; pace: 4.5 mph

HEART RATE: 70–80% of maximum

COOL-DOWN: 5–7 minutes after walk stretches

FREQUENCY: 3–5 times per week

WEEKLY MILEAGE: 12–20 miles

ORANGE/RED MAINTENANCE PROGRAM

WARM-UP: 5–7 minutes before walk stretches

AEROBIC WORK OUT: mileage: 4.0; pace: 4.5 mph
weight/incline: Add weights to upper body or add hill walking as needed to keep heart rate in target zone (70–80% of predicted maximum).

HEART RATE: 70–80% of maximum

COOL-DOWN: 5–7 minutes after walk stretches

FREQUENCY: 3–5 times per week

WEEKLY MILEAGE: 12–20 miles

41

FIGURE 6
Determining Target Heart Rate Zone

Age	Average Maximum Heart Rate (beats/minute)	Target Training Zone (beats/minute) 60%	80%	70% Maximum Heart Rate (beats/minute)
20	200	120	160	140
25	195	117	156	137
30	190	114	152	133
35	185	111	148	130
40	180	108	144	126
45	175	105	140	123
50	170	102	136	119
55	165	99	132	116
60	160	96	128	112
65	155	93	124	109
70	150	90	120	105

upper end of his target training zone. Now you have all the information you need to tailor-make a fitness program and to put it into action.

At the end of each twenty-week program, retest yourself with RFWT just as you did at the beginning. From this test, gauge your progress, and on the basis of your second result start another program. Repeat the whole process every twenty weeks until you reach the fitness level you want. Once you have reached the Yellow, Red, or Orange level of fitness and are satisfied with the way you feel, then you can adopt the Yellow or Red or Orange maintenance program for a lifetime of fitness.

For optimal benefits follow each program carefully and don't skip any of the phases of the program. The major advantage of adhering to this fitness-walking schedule is that it is carefully designed to begin with a degree of difficulty suited to your aerobic capacity and to increase in difficulty as your aerobic capacity improves.

Testing Yourself for Fitness Walking on a Treadmill

Fitness walking on a treadmill is becoming increasingly popular. Walking on a treadmill carries all the physiological and health benefits of walking outside. One disadvantage of walking on a treadmill is that you are not outside enjoying the sun, breeze, smells, and sights. A significant advantage, however, is that treadmill walking can be done regardless of what the weather is like outside. Many of our patients and research subjects find that either owning a treadmill or belonging to a health club that has treadmills helps them maintain their walking program—particularly during the extremely cold or hot weather.

Another advantage of treadmill walking is that in addition to controlling speed you can control the angle of the treadmill, thus giving yourself a permanent hill to walk up if you want to increase the intensity of your walking session.

In 1989, our laboratory expanded the concept of the original Rockport Fitness Walking Test to allow you to utilize a similar test on the treadmill to test yourself for fitness walking. The new test, called the Rockport® Fitness Treadmill Test™, is very easy to take. It has been scientifically validated in our laboratory and shown to be as accurate as the original test.

The treadmill test is very similar to the original test which was developed for walking on a track. Stretch and warm up in the same way that has already been described in this chapter. To warm up on the treadmill, start by walking at a slow speed for a few minutes and gradually increase your

FIGURE 7

Relative Fitness Levels and Exercise Programs for the Rockport Fitness Treadmill Test

20- to 29-Year-Old Males
Relative Fitness Level

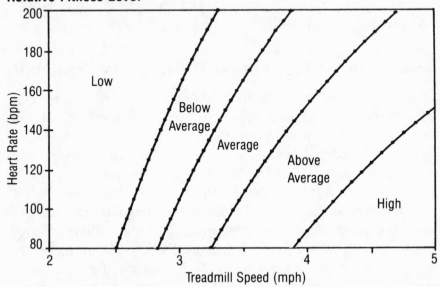

20- to 29-Year-Old Males
Exercise Program

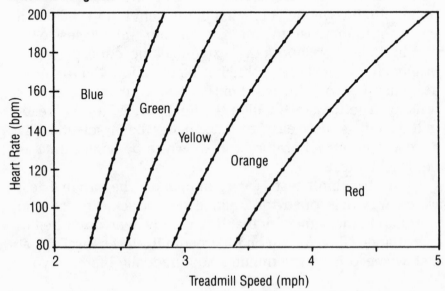

20- to 29-Year-Old Females
Relative Fitness Level

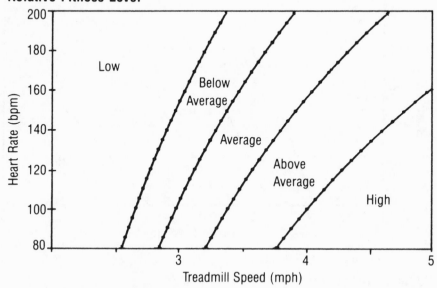

20- to 29-Year-Old Females
Exercise Program

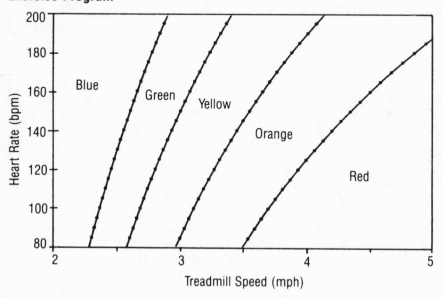

30- to 39-Year-Old Males
Relative Fitness Level

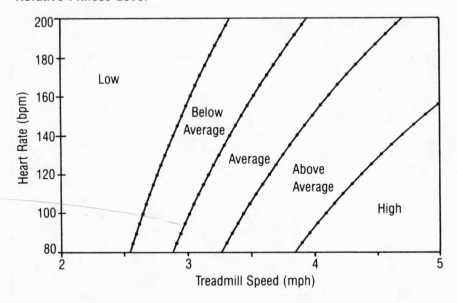

30- to 39-Year-Old Males
Exercise Program

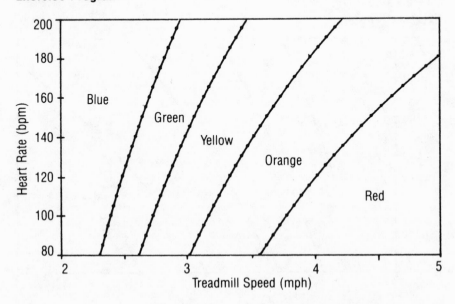

30- to 39-Year-Old Females
Relative Fitness Level

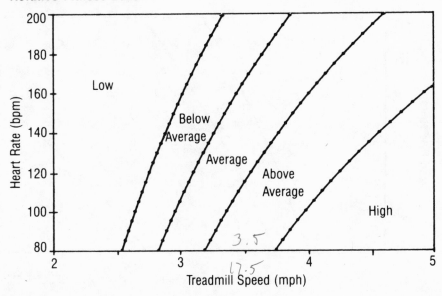

30- to 39-Year-Old Females
Exercise Program

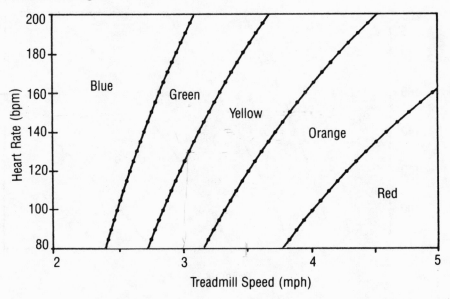

40- to 49-Year-Old Males
Relative Fitness Level

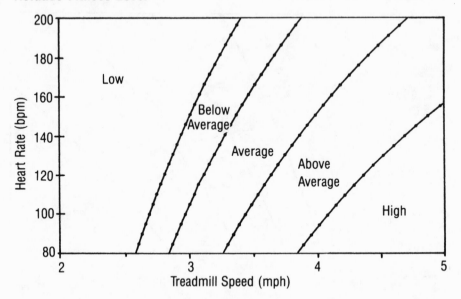

40- to 49-Year-Old Males
Exercise Program

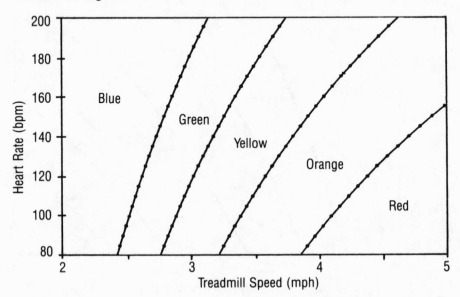

40- to 49-Year-Old Females
Relative Fitness Level

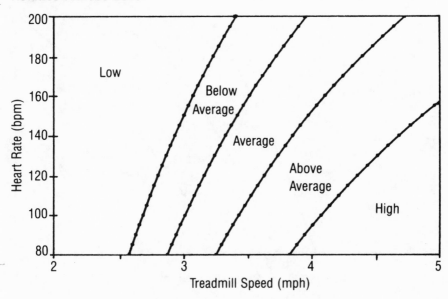

40- to 49-Year-Old Females
Exercise Program

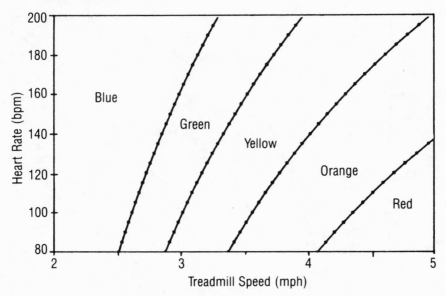

50- to 59-Year-Old Males
Relative Fitness Level

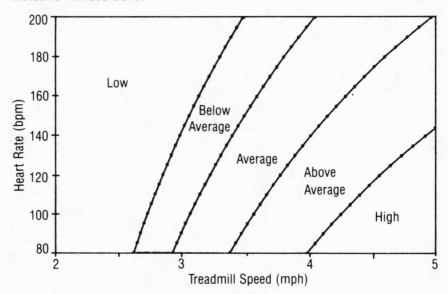

50- to 59-Year-Old Males
Exercise Program

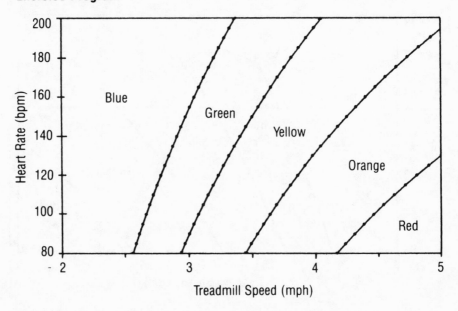

50- to 59-Year-Old Females
Relative Fitness Level

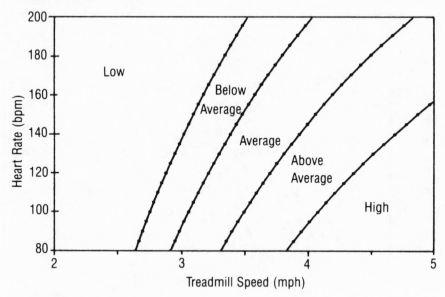

50- to 59-Year-Old Females
Exercise Program

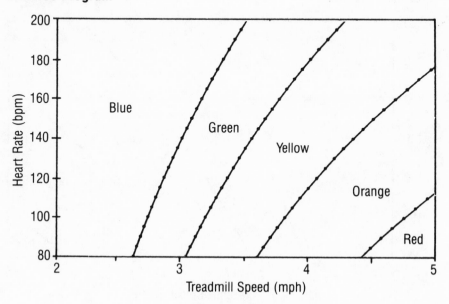

**60- to 69-Year-Old Males
Relative Fitness Level**

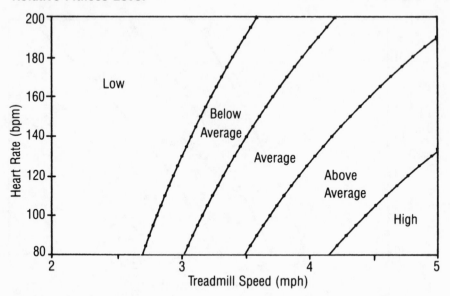

**60- to 69-Year-Old Males
Exercise Program**

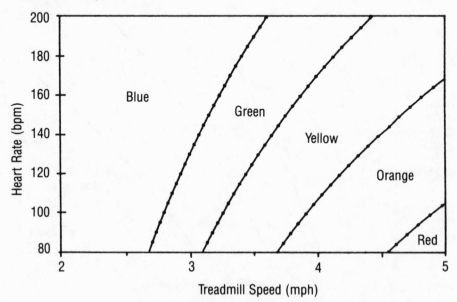

60- to 69-Year-Old Females
Relative Fitness Level

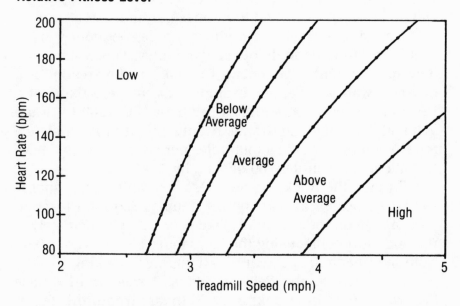

60- to 69-Year-Old Females
Exercise Program

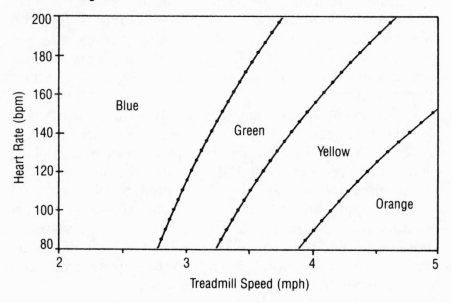

speed until you have reached a "brisk" speed, but one that you feel you can maintain for a mile. For most people this will be between three and four miles per hour.

Now simply divide the number of miles per hour you are walking on the treadmill into sixty minutes. This will tell you how many minutes you need to walk on the treadmill in order to walk a mile. For example, if you are walking at a treadmill speed of three miles per hour, divide 60 by 3 and you find that you need to walk twenty minutes to complete a mile. If you were walking four miles per hour, you would have to walk fifteen minutes (60 divided by 4).

To take the Rockport® Fitness Treadmill Test™ simply walk the appropriate number of minutes required to complete a mile on the treadmill. Take your pulse immediately at the end of the mile, using the techniques already described. Note the treadmill speed at which you were walking.

Now refer to the Relative Fitness Levels and Exercise Programs for the Rockport® Fitness Treadmill Test™ (Figure 7). Find the appropriate charts for your age and sex. Draw a vertical line from the treadmill speed you used and a horizontal line from your heart rate at the end of the mile. When this is done on the Relative Fitness Chart, it tells you how you compare to other individuals of your age and sex. When this is done on the Exercise Program Chart for your age and sex, it tells you which exercise program to start on the treadmill.

The exercise programs are identical to those for the Rockport Fitness Walking Test, which have already been described in this chapter. For example, if your results place you in the Green Exercise Program, it is the same for both the original walk test and for the treadmill walking test.

The odds are that if you exercise regularly for six months, you will continue to exercise for the rest of your life. You need to find the program that is right for you, discipline yourself for a few months, keep track of your progress, and allow walking to become a habit for life.

3

THE SPORT FOR ALL
AMERICANS

Walking for Aerobic Fitness

While we were developing the Rockport Fitness Walking Test, one volunteer who works at the medical center returned five times to try the test because he was sure he could do better. He was right. Every time he took the test, he got faster. Finally he walked a mile in less than nine minutes—faster than the average person jogs. While that set a record for our lab, it wasn't even close to the world's record for walking the indoor mile, which is five minutes and forty-one seconds—faster than most people run. All this should convince even the most stubborn detractors of walking that it can be a vigorous form of exercise.

From our laboratory experiments we've learned that walking is an excellent aerobic conditioner. *Aerobic* literally means "in the presence of air." Aerobic exercise strengthens the cardiovascular system by using the body's large muscle groups in a repetitive fashion; the system of aerobic pathways—whose function is to combine air with glucose to generate energy—thus works a little harder than it does when it's at rest. Over time the additional work associated with aerobic exercise makes the system stronger and more efficient, and when exercise is done consistently over a lifetime it reduces the risk of developing coronary heart disease.

During the fitness boom of the last few years, people have often confused short-term training, such as athletes undergo, with staying active for long-term cardiovascular health. When athletes prepare for competitions, they undergo a specific program of sustained, intense exercise designed to train their cardiovascular systems to work harder and more efficiently to achieve a specific athletic goal.

If you train vigorously for three months and then quit, you haven't improved your chances of preventing heart disease. A college or Olympic athlete who becomes sedentary after stopping competition soon becomes as susceptible to heart disease as any other sedentary person. Consistency is essential to an exercise program designed to lower your risk of heart disease by improving your aerobic system.

Conditioning is complicated, because the body has two sources of energy, described as *aerobic* and *anaerobic.* The aerobic system produces more than 90 percent of the body's energy needs both at rest and during moderate exercise. It is the far more efficient of the two systems. The anaerobic system generates energy in the absence of oxygen. Using fuel stored in the muscles, this system supplies most of the energy required during the first minute of exercise and during the short bursts of intense exertion needed to do such activities as sprinting, lifting weights, or throwing a discus. The aerobic pathways simply can't supply the body's need fast enough. Though the anaerobic system creates energy quickly in these short-term situations, it does so much less efficiently than the aerobic system, creating the extra energy but generating considerable waste. One waste product is lactic acid, which can make your muscles feel sore.

Let's see how this works when you walk. As you start your walk and the exercising muscles begin to contract and expend energy, they call on your heart and lungs to deliver more oxygen-rich blood for fuel. The heart takes forty-five to ninety seconds to deliver enough oxygenated blood to the muscles to meet the requirements of the exercise. Meantime, your muscles must use the local supply of energy while your body shifts gears up from the anaerobic system to the aerobic system. You may feel a little sluggish and leaden during the first several minutes of your walk as your muscles are waiting for the aerobic system to catch up with the demand. One way to ease the transition from anaerobic to aerobic is to warm up and increase your pace gradually.

If the walking program you are engaged in is appropriate for your age, sex, and level of fitness, your aerobic pathways will produce 90 percent of the energy you use after two or three minutes. Unless you increase your pace, it continues to do so. As you slow down at the end of your walk, your energy production gradually decreases. For a few minutes after you have finished exercising, however, your energy consumption remains high, in part to repay some of the "oxygen debt" the anaerobic system used as you started your walk.

As you begin your fitness-walking regime, keep in mind that stretching, warming up, and cooling down are essential parts of an aerobic walking routine. Abrupt strenuous exercise is uncomfortable because it demands intense work from the anaerobic system, which in turn produces a lot of waste and can make your muscles sore. Warmed-up muscles and tendons are more resilient and become less tired and sore. Cooling down also helps prevent stiffness because it allows the muscles to clear themselves of waste products as blood vessels slowly constrict and blood flow is gradually redirected.

Before and after your walk, you should stretch for five to ten minutes to loosen muscles and tendons and prevent injuries. Specific guidelines and stretches are described in chapter 9.

After stretching, warm up by walking slowly and increasing your pace gradually for the first quarter of a mile before beginning your timed walk. At the end of your walk, cool down by gradually slowing your pace for the last quarter of a mile. Repeat the stretches at the end of your walk. You may actually think of these as the beginning and ending parts of a three-phase exercise session. In the warm-up period your heart rate gradually accelerates to the target heart rate training zone. In the aerobic phase your heart beats in the target heart-rate training zone, where most of the cardiovascular health benefits occur. In the cool-down phase your heart rate slowly decreases to the resting state. All three phases are necessary for safe and effective aerobic conditioning.

Walking for Women

Since educational sports programs for women have traditionally been less strenuous and less competitive than those for men, many older women who had never been very physically active were left cold by the running craze of the seventies. The stress and pounding of running put them off this approach to fitness. But today older women are becoming increasingly aware of the need for exercise.

Younger women may find they have little time for exercise between working at a full-time job, keeping house, and taking care of their children. Teenage girls often carry more pounds and bulges than they would like, but many are reluctant to start a fitness program. It's just not the thing to do.

The best time for a woman to begin walking is when she's young. You establish a habit of exercise that can last a lifetime, increasing the quality and length of your life. If you are unhappy with your body and insecure about yourself, then fitness walking is the perfect exercise for you. It helps you to lose weight, enhances your self-esteem, and gives you greater self-confidence.

Walking promises help for women of all ages. For the older woman, our fitness-walking program banishes the "no pain, no gain" theory of sports while providing cardio-vascular health.

Walking also helps women avoid or slow the process of osteoporosis. This condition afflicts more than 15 million Americans and is responsible for many hip fractures and broken bones in the elderly. Women are far more susceptible to osteoporosis than men. Because they begin with lighter bones, there is less bulk for them to lose. At menopause the production of estrogen—which has helped keep their bones strong—is reduced drastically. The loss of estrogen aggra-vates the natural loss of bone mass with aging. If women exercise, however, their bones, like their muscles, grow stronger. The best way to slow the process of osteoporosis is to exercise and to take estrogen replacement and calcium (if your doctor recommends them).

For the hurried woman with many commitments to work, home, and family, walking can be a time for enjoying children and friends. You can carry your tiny baby in a soft pack on your chest or in a metal-frame backpack when he or she gets bigger. Children love this, and it is good for them. Investigators in England found that babies carried close to their mothers were less fussy and more contented than babies who didn't go for walks with their mothers. Taking a friend along on your walk or going with a group of people is also pleasant. In fact, walking can be a great social activity.

Walking for People Over Fifty

According to the Census Bureau, on July 20, 1988, America was silently transformed. It officially shifted from a youth culture to a "graying" society. On that day the number of people in the United States between the ages of thirty-five and sixty-five exceeded for the first time the number of people between the ages of eighteen and thirty-four. There are now more people over the age of sixty-five than there are teenagers, and this trend will continue. By the year 2010, baby boomers will be over sixty.

This fact is not lost on some of America's most influential and powerful individuals. We recently surveyed 1,130 CEOs, including 128 CEOs of the Fortune 500 companies. Their average age was fifty-five. Amazingly, 65 percent of them exercised daily. Among these business people, running and fitness walking almost tied for first place as favorite exercises. One of the CEOs observed that after age fifty people either have established a regular exercise program or they tend not to exercise at all.

Those executives who exercised regularly believed they were not only protecting their health but were also maintaining their energy and reducing stress. Donald Lennox, former chief executive of Navistar, walked briskly for two or three miles from his apartment to his office. He said, "I build up a good head of steam and by the time I get in here, I'm ready to work with no tendency to doze off." A majority of these successful people make time to exercise because their jobs as well as their private lives demand that they maintain their energy and strength.

Researchers who have studied the physical condition of people in their fifties, sixties, and seventies are convinced that many of the conditions we thought were caused by age or illness are, in fact, the result of inactivity. Obesity—which increases after the age of fifty—probably can be blamed at least as much on inactivity as on eating too many calories. Osteoporosis can be slowed through a walking program. Although aerobic capacity and strength decline somewhat with age, major studies have indicated that most of the decline probably results from inactivity.

One study showed that maximum oxygen consumption declined in sedentary men three times as fast as it did in active men. Another recent study demonstrated that active seventy-year-old women more closely resembled twenty-year-old women in strength, balance, and reaction time than they did inactive seventy-year-olds. A study performed in our laboratory found that it's never too late to begin a walking program, because older adults benefit as much as younger people do from exercise. In our study of individuals between the ages of seventy and seventy-nine, a twelve-week program of fitness walking resulted in an average gain in aerobic capacity of 12 percent, comparable to what we typically see in a much younger population.

When elderly people have been sedentary for a long time, many everyday tasks become difficult. They may have problems getting out of a car or a bathtub or a soft chair. They can have difficulty reaching to screw in a light bulb or stooping to pick up a quarter. Fitness can be defined as the ability to do what we need to do to get along in our environment. Physical activity becomes a way to maintain the strength, flexibility, and balance we need to get along in our daily life and to remain independent and self-sufficient.

Fitness walking is an excellent path to take to fitness if you are over fifty, but there are a few basic facts that you should consider before you begin.

• Since connective tissue becomes stiffer as you age, it's particularly important that you stretch and loosen up before you exercise.

• Don't expect one week of frantic activity to undo what ten years of inactivity have done. Following the fitness-walking programs described in Chapter 2 can help you avoid overdoing it.

• Get proper walking shoes because they will protect the connective tissue by supporting and cushioning your feet as you walk.

• If you have been sedentary for over a year, check with your physician to be sure there is nothing that will prevent you from walking for fitness. If you know your physician, this may involve nothing more than a phone call. If you don't have a physician, find one who is interested in physical fitness and walking and in helping you get into better shape.

4

PRACTICAL CONSIDERATIONS

Weather

The weather may be one of your chief obstacles in fitness walking. While spring and fall are pleasant and agreeable for outdoor activities in almost all parts of the country, in many places the winter and summer weather can make your walk uncomfortable and even unsafe. Of course, when weather conditions are extreme, you should find a place to walk indoors.

In the summer, at times of high heat and humidity, observe some practical precautions:

1. Wear lightweight, light-colored, loose-fitting, absorbent clothing.

2. Give your body time to become accustomed to hot weather, gradually increasing the time you spend walking in the heat. It may take as long as two weeks.

3. Walk in the early morning or in the evening. Not only is the sun hotter during the middle of the day, but there is also radiant heat from the pavement or the ground.

4. Hydration is crucial, so drink lots of water before, during, and after your walk. Don't wait till you feel thirsty.

5. Don't push yourself. Walk slower to keep your heart rate in its normal range. This is especially important for seniors and cardiac patients.

6. Cardiac patients and older people who have not been exercising should be especially careful.

7. The warning signs of heat stress include headache, dizziness, fatigue, muscle cramps, and an absence of perspiration. At the first signs, get out of the heat, drink water, and rest.

As the saying goes, "It's not the heat, it's the humidity." The likelihood of heat stress increases as the relative humidity goes up. For example, when the temperature is 85 degrees and the humidity is 50 percent there is little danger, but if the relative humidity rises to 100 percent and the temperature remains the same, there is a risk of heat stroke. So don't just look at the thermometer, consider the humidity as well. To find out if heat and humidity pose a problem on any particular day, check Figure 8.

In cold weather, it takes some determination to exercise outside, but the challenge of the cold often adds a spring to your step and makes you feel especially alert and alive. As long as you are wary about certain hazards, you can enjoy your walk in the wintertime. Just remember the following advice, as offered by Madeline Drexler in *The Walking Magazine* (Dec./Jan. 1988).

1. Dress in layers to suit the temperature. Avoid tight clothes. Loose clothing traps layers of air and provides good insulation.

2. Start your walk into the wind and return with the wind at your back. This way you won't get chilled by the sweat you've worked up.

FIGURE 8
Heat Stress Index

Relative humidity plays tricks on your body. In the summer it can make you feel much hotter than the actual temperature, and it escalates the likelihood of heat stress. For example, if you go walking when the air temperature is a tolerable 85°F, with humidity at 90%, it is equivalent to exercising at 102°F. The chart below shows how this works for a range of temperatures and humidity levels. Shaded areas indicate points where exertion may be dangerous.

AIR TEMPERATURE (F°)

		70°	75°	80°	85°	90°	95°	100°	105°	110°	115°	120°
RELATIVE HUMIDITY	30%	67	73	78	84	90	96	104	113	123	135	148
	40%	68	74	79	86	93	101	110	123	137	151	
	50%	69	75	81	88	96	107	120	135	150		
	60%	70	76	82	90	100	114	132	149			
	70%	70	77	85	93	106	124	144				
	80%	71	78	86	97	113	136					
	90%	71	79	88	102	122						
	100%	72	80	91	108							

☐ Risk of heat exhaustion   ☐ Risk of heat stroke   ■ High risk of heat stroke

3. For greater stability on ice and snow, walk in a wider gait, turning your toes outward slightly.

4. Shoes with cushion soles or cleats are better than shoes with metal studs, which get slippery when they wear smooth.

5. Hands, nose, and ears are especially vulnerable to frostbite and should be covered if the temperature is below freezing and if it is windy.

6. Hypothermia—low body temperature—is a very dangerous condition and can occur even when the temperature is above freezing if you get wet or are not dressed warmly. The symptoms are disorientation, sluggishness, slurred speech, and a stumbling gait. If you feel any of these symptoms, get out of the cold as quickly as possible and have a warm drink. In the winter, always walk where there are plenty of other people so that if you should fall, someone will see you.

7. Women lose heat faster than men, and thin people faster than fat people, so be aware that you and your walking companions can reach the point of hypothermia at very different rates.

8. People with high blood pressure should dress especially warmly to avoid shivering, which elevates blood pressure.

9. You don't catch cold from the cold weather, and there's no harm in walking outdoors when you have a cold, provided you don't have a fever.

Just as the relative humidity makes hot temperatures more stressful, the wind increases the effect of lower temperatures. Weathermen often refer to this as the "wind-chill factor," and when they report on the temperature they take the wind into account. You should, too. To find out if wind chill poses a problem on any particular day, see Figure 9.

Gear

One great advantage of fitness walking is that it doesn't require equipment—no uniforms, bats, balls, rackets, skis, helmets, or gloves. But you *will* need a good pair of walking shoes.

With the development of high-speed video equipment and powerful personal computers, a new branch of science called biomechanics has studied in minute detail the forces and motions of the body that occur in any physical activity. Given that information, engineers have been able to design better, safer, and higher-performance athletic equipment (rear-entry ski boots, graphite tennis rackets, and running shoes that protect runners from shin splints are a few examples).

Walking shoes, too, have profited from technological advances. Though you may have been walking all your life without any special shoes, when you begin fitness walking, you make greater demands on your feet than ever before,

FIGURE 9

Wind Speed and Temperature Chart

The wind-chill factor (Equivalent Temperature) on any particular day is the point where the line for Air Temperature (reading from top to bottom) intersects with the line for Wind Speed (reading from left to right). The different zones show when the combination of cold weather and wind makes it unsafe to walk.

ESTIMATED WIND SPEED (MPH)	AIR TEMPERATURE (°F)									
	50	40	30	20	10	0	−10	−20	−30	−40
	EQUIVALENT TEMPERATURE (°F)									
Calm	50	40	30	20	10	0	−10	−20	−30	−40
5	48	37	27	16	6	−5	−15	−26	−36	−47
10	40	28	16	4	−9	−21	−33	−46	−58	−70
15	36	22	9	−5	−18	−36	−45	−58	−72	−85
20	32	18	4	−10	−25	−39	−53	−67	−82	−96
25	30	16	0	−15	−29	−44	−59	−74	−88	−104
30	28	13	−2	−18	−33	−48	−63	−79	−94	−109
35	27	11	−4	−20	−35	−49	−67	−83	−98	−113
40	26	10	−6	−21	−37	−53	−69	−85	−100	−116

Wind speeds over 40 mph have little additional effect

Little danger for properly clothed person

Increasing danger
DANGER OF FREEZING EXPOSED FLESH

Great danger

Temperatures assume dry conditions. The greater the moisture, the higher the temperature at which your skin may be in danger.

Reprinted with permission of *The Walking Magazine*, March 1987; © 1987, Raben Publishing Co., 711 Boyelston St., Boston, MA 02116.

and you need shoes designed to meet those special demands (Figure 10).

Contrary to popular belief, walking is not simply running at a slower speed, and a good running shoe does not necessarily make a good walking shoe. A careful study in our biomechanics laboratory showed that the motion of walking is very different from the motion of running. The angle at which the heel hits the ground is sharper in walking, and the

FIGURE 10 _____

ProWalker™ 9000/2300 Series

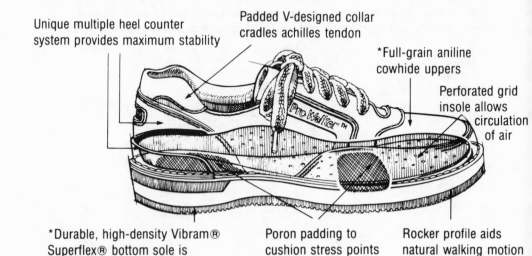

Unique multiple heel counter system provides maximum stability

Padded V-designed collar cradles achilles tendon

*Full-grain aniline cowhide uppers

Perforated grid insole allows circulation of air

*Durable, high-density Vibram® Superflex® bottom sole is ribbed for slip resistance

Poron padding to cushion stress points

Rocker profile aids natural walking motion

*Available in some styles

Illustration courtesy The Rockport Company

transfer of weight is not at all the same. In walking, you land on your heel, slowly roll the weight forward onto the toes of your foot, then push off with your toes, all the while maintaining contact with the ground. In running, you land on your heel then rapidly transfer the weight from the heel to the toes and leap off the ground with every stride. Whereas running shoes need to be soft enough to cushion the impact of landing after these leaps and flexible enough to allow for the rapid transfer of weight from heel to toes, walking shoes need to be firmer to support the weight during that slower rolling motion of the foot.

Your shoes must perform two functions: They must cushion impact and allow for transfer of weight from heel to toes, and they must control excessive motion as the foot hits the ground. In running shoes the first function is more important; in walking shoes both functions are equally important.

When walking, 95 percent of people land on the outside of their heel and roll their weight toward the inside of the heel; the other 5 percent land on the inside of their heel and rotate to the outside. The outside-to-inside motion on the striking of the heel is called *pronation,* and it helps to brake your forward motion. While a little pronation is a desirable part of the braking process, too much pronation is a problem. It produces excess torque that moves up through every joint of the leg, and this can tire ankles, knees, and hips and can even strain or injure those joints.

A good shoe must be firm enough to control excess pronation, but it also must be soft enough to cushion impact—functions that are sometimes at cross purposes. Soft materials that cushion impact are not necessarily the best materials to control motion. Fortunately, we now have walking shoes that have been carefully designed to do an excellent job of both. In a biomechanics test of walking at four miles per hour, well-designed walking shoes performed equally as well as tennis shoes, aerobic dance shoes, running shoes, and cross-training shoes in cushioning impact and were far superior to any of these other shoes in controlling pronation. And, by the way, some companies are now incorporating many of the features of walking shoes in dress shoes as well. Don't accept the notion that your feet must be uncomfortable even when you wear dress shoes. Even women's dress pumps are beginning to incorporate biomechanically improved designs for more comfortable walking.

Here are some specific features you should look for in your fitness-walking shoe:

• They should be lightweight, because any extra weight you carry for a number of miles will be tiring.
• The upper part of the shoe should be sturdy, preferably constructed of leather or mesh, which will give your foot plenty of support.
• They should have a roomy toe box, because your toes spread out when your foot hits the ground and during the push-off.
• The heel should be slightly lower than the toe to allow the weight to shift from heel to toe in a rocker motion.
• The shoes should have a special cup in the heel, called a heel counter, to control pronation. Some walking shoes have two heel counters, one internal and one external.
• The shoes should have an internal orthotic support structure to cradle the foot and hold it in the proper position throughout the walking stride.

When you purchase walking shoes, put them on and walk around the shoe store at the same pace you intend to walk outside. If the shoe feels too cushiony, it may not have enough support for fitness walking.

Here is a glossary of terms that Susanna Levin compiled for *The Walking Magazine* (Jan. 1987). Knowing these terms will enable you to ask for what you want and understand what the salesperson in the shoe store is talking about.

Collar. The opening of the shoe where you put your foot in.

Counter or **heel counter.** The cup at the back of the inside of the shoe that wraps around the heel and provides lateral (outside) and medial (inside) stability.

Dual density, triple density. The combination or layering of materials of different densities (degrees of firmness) in the sole. Soft materials add cushioning, firm materials add stability and durability.

EVA. Ethylene vinyl acetate, a lightweight and soft material often used as cushioning in the midsoles of walking shoes.

Footbed. A molded insole including arch support, heel support, and cushioning.

Heel cradle. The part of the footbed surrounding the base of the heel that adds comfort and stability.

Heel cup or **stabilizer cup.** Also called a heel counter or heel cradle. This is added to the inside of the heel of a shoe for extra cushioning and protection.

Heel cushion. Any feature of the footbed designed to absorb shock to the heel.

Heel stabilizer. An external device that controls pronation in the rear foot.

Insert. A removable insole or footbed.

Insole. The insert or a sock lining that the foot rests on.

Last. The form or mold over which the shoe is shaped.

Midsole. The soft cushioning material between the insole and the bottom sole of the shoe.

Motion-control device. A strip of polyurethane or nylon wrapped around the outside of the heel to stabilize pronation.

Notched heel. A dip in the back of the collar to prevent pressure on the Achilles tendon.

Orthotic. A type of footbed shaped by a podiatrist from a cast of an individual's foot. Sometimes this term is used to describe footbeds designed to conform to the foot as the shoe is worn.

Outsole. The bottom of the shoe that touches the ground. A flared outsole (sometimes called a flared midsole) found on running shoes widens below the foot for stability.

Saddle. Reinforcement over the top of the shoe near the laces for added arch support and stability.

Shank. A strip of firm material between the insole and the midsole that runs from the ball of the foot to the heel to provide arch support.

Sock lining. The soft top layer of an insole that has no shape.

Upper. The top part of the shoe, generally made of nylon, canvas, or leather.

Wedge. The thick part of the midsole that makes the heel higher than the ball of the foot.

Never wear your walking shoes without socks. The perspiration from your feet can harm your shoes, and you will almost certainly develop blisters if you fitness-walk. In warm weather socks made of cotton or a blend of cotton and Orlon will help keep your feet comfortable and blister-free by wicking the perspiration away while you walk.

Aside from shoes and socks, all other walking gear is optional, though some walkers think carrying a walking stick improves their balance and helps protect them from unfriendly dogs.

Over the last few years walkers have found certain kinds of clothing particularly suitable for fitness walking. In moderate weather many people like to wear sweats made of knitted cotton or cotton blend with a fleecy inside. They are comfortable, allow great mobility, and absorb perspiration.

For cooler weather or rainy weather short of a downpour, a nylon windbreaker and nylon warm-up pants are ideal. If you want to, you can add a sweater underneath the windbreaker. In really stormy weather, you can wear water-repellent clothing. Beware of raingear that does not "breathe." If air cannot circulate, you will find yourself as wet from your own perspiration as you would be from the rain. A jacket and pants made of a fabric like Gore-Tex or Ultrex, which allow water vapor to escape but prevent moisture from getting in, are ideal. To keep your feet dry, choose shoes or boots lined with Gore-Tex.

In cold weather the rule is: Dress in layers. Here's what the U.S. Army prescribes for soldiers in cold weather:

1. Next to your skin wear long underwear.

2. The second layer should be a garment made of wool knit, synthetic pile, or fleece (a sweatshirt, for example). This layer can be removed if you get too hot.

3. On top wear a jacket lined with a waterproof breathable fabric such as Gore-Tex or Ultrex.

The object is to keep you warm and dry from perspiration as well as the elements. Clothes heavy with moisture from perspiration can chill you twenty-five times faster than normal. Natural fibers—cotton, wool, and silk—all have their advantages. And manufacturers have been hard at work developing man-made fibers to suit all conditions.

Wet or dry, wool is an excellent insulator because it absorbs and holds moisture. Woolen underwear, however, isn't recommended for race walkers or power striders. The trapped moisture makes the fabric heavy. And while perspiration-dampened wool underwear will keep you warm as long as you are moving and generating heat, once you stop, the soggy surface becomes very chilly.

Cotton feels wonderful against your skin, but it doesn't insulate as well as wool or silk. It absorbs moisture, so it's a good idea to wear it on days when the temperature is above freezing. Cotton is often blended with polyester in a fishnet weave that holds pockets of insulating air next to your skin. For *maximum* protection, wear fishnet weave under other underwear. Cotton blended with wool is highly thermal and feels comfortable against the skin.

Silk is lightweight and comfortable and an excellent insulator, properties that make it particularly good for recreational fitness walking.

Besides these natural fibers, there are many high-tech fabrics. Polyester fibers are light in weight and good insulators, but they repel water (and perspiration) unless they are specially treated. Capilene and Thermax are polyester fibers specially treated so that the outer surface absorbs moisture and then forces it to spread out so it can dry rapidly through the outer layers of clothes. These materials can be cared for easily. Polypropylene is extremely lightweight and a good insulator that also pushes moisture into the outer garments to dry, but it tends to retain body odor. Check the label for laundering instructions.

Then there are fabrics that are really layers of fabrics bonded together. One of the latest has an inside layer of brushed polyester that draws moisture away from the skin into an outside layer of Hydrofil nylon. Some of these layered fabrics are designed for specific temperatures, which can be helpful if you know the kind of weather to expect. The heaviest of them is designed for low-activity sports like fishing or hunting and may be too bulky and too hot for fitness walking.

Doctors speak of the "rule of ten": You lose 10 percent of your heat through your feet, 10 percent through your head, and 10 percent through your hands. That's why a hat, gloves, and warm socks are crucial during cold weather. To keep your feet warm, wear two pairs of socks—the inner pair of some insulating fiber, the outer pair of wool. Your hands are particularly susceptible to cold temperatures because blood leaves the extremities to heat the body's core in cold weather. To protect your fingers, wear mittens instead of gloves, because air circulates in mittens and they retain heat better. Wool mittens with a wind-resistant outer shell are ideal.

Other than clothing, there are several pieces of equipment you may want to consider.

If you want to bring your baby along for your walk, carrying him or her in a pack on your chest or back frees your hands and arms to swing with your stride.

Carrying a pocketbook will hinder your arm swing and your stride, so put whatever you need in your pockets or consider buying a waist belt, fanny pack, or any of the other types of packs available in which to carry keys, glasses, snacks, windbreaker, or whatever you think you will need for your walk.

A pedometer helps you keep track of how far you have come by counting your paces and the miles you have covered. There are many types; some only tell you the number of miles while others give you miles and fractions. Pedometers rely on your stride length, so pay close attention to this to avoid inaccuracies.

Injury Prevention

While walking is one of the safest sports, walkers are still susceptible to strains and stresses to the legs and feet. You can avoid many problems by wearing sturdy, well-fitted shoes and lightweight socks made of a breathable fiber. Although more than 60 percent of foot problems are probably due to inherited traits, shoes often aggravate the situation. Many other problems are minor and can be treated with a little careful first aid. The best advice, however, is to prevent injuries before they occur. If you have foot problems to start with or develop one, consult your local podiatrist.

Blisters, probably the most common foot problem, can ruin a fine day's walk. Blisters result from friction and begin as a hot spot. If you stop and put a Band-aid on the spot, you may avoid a full-fledged blister. If the hot spot remains unattended and the friction continues, a fluid-filled sac forms between the inner dermal layer of skin and the epidermis to protect the inner layer from irritation. Besides correct shoes, the best preventives are powder and lubricants. You may want to rub a thin coat of petroleum jelly over the ball of your foot then apply another light coat on the outside of the sock. To avoid staining socks and the inside of your shoe you can use water-based or silicon lubricants.

Moleskin may be useful in preventing blisters if you cover a hot spot before it turns into a full-fledged blister. But adhesive-backed products like moleskin can pull off the top layer of skin once the blister has formed. Use pads without adhesive to protect full-fledged blisters. Opening a blister to drain the fluid remains a questionable procedure. We do not recommend this practice since it can lead to infection.

Calluses are thick accumulations of dead skin cells that build up over tender skin to protect it from irritation. There is no need to treat calluses unless they hurt. If you have a callus that is causing trouble, use a pumice stone or callus file and a lotion of 10 percent urea or anhydrous lanolin to break down the callus; then you can scrub it away.

Do not use a razor or pads with salicylic acid. The acid can spread to the surrounding skin and cause a more serious problem. This can be especially dangerous if you are a diabetic or have circulatory problems.

When feet, ankles, or tendons become sore from over-use, the first line of defense is to make sure you have good walking shoes. The only other remedy is to cut back a little in the distances you are walking.

Aching arches are a common problem for athletes and exercisers. The ache comes from pounding your feet on the ground. It may help to use removable arch supports or orthotic supports in your shoes, but if aching does develop, use cold packs to reduce inflammation and rest your feet. Massage has a soothing effect.

Sprains result from violent stretching of the ligaments. (Ligaments attach bones to other bones.) If you stumble or twist your ankle or knee, walk on it gingerly for a little while. You're probably all right if the pain subsides after a few minutes. If it still hurts, you should discontinue your walk. Should the soreness get worse or last more than twenty-four hours, you should consider seeing a doctor.

Sprains can be ranked from first to third degree and can be judged by the severity of the swelling and pain. Minor first-degree sprains involve stretching and a little tearing of one or more ligaments. If you heard a popping sound when you stumbled, then you probably suffered a second- or third-degree sprain and need to see a doctor. In second-degree sprains the tear in the ligament is major but the whole ligament is not torn in two. In third-degree sprains—which are often worse than fractures—the whole joint is dislocated and the ligaments are totally severed.

The immediate first aid to minimize the damage of a sprain is known by the acronym RICE:

Rest for the ankle or knee, which means staying off it as much as possible.

Ice to reduce the swelling.

Compress the joint by wrapping it in an Ace bandage.

Elevate the joint to decrease blood flow and reduce pain and swelling.

Since a serious sprain stretches and damages ligaments forever, sprained joints are vulnerable to reinjury. During rehabilitation, work to strengthen the muscles around the ligaments to help them reinforce the weakened joint. Walking as soon as your injured joint will bear your weight is the best way to strengthen the joint. Work up slowly and stop when it hurts.

Where to Walk

The paths you choose for your walk can run the gamut from a mall to a swamp, depending on where you live and what you like to see as you're walking. One of the very best ways to motivate yourself is to make the walk enjoyable. If you are beginning to lose interest in your program, one of the first remedies is to change your course.

Janet, a volunteer in one of our studies, made a game of charting her entire neighborhood. She drove around charting two-mile, three-mile, and four-mile loops and laid out her map of places to walk for several weeks in advance. She found that by varying the route she met different people, saw different sights, and enjoyed her walk more. Even charting the route was interesting. Stephen Graham, an English writer, liked to do zigzag walking in cities, turning left at one intersection and right at another, creating a random route that brought him many surprises. Other people prefer the familiar. They like to watch the seasons change at the same pond or hillside. In the city many walkers enjoy a park, but others find a sidewalk with pedestrians more interesting.

It's worth the effort to plan a new route before the old one becomes dull. Some of the changes can be very simple. If you usually walk near your home, try walking near where you work instead. If you always walk outside but find the weather beginning to get unpleasant, move indoors for the winter or the summer. More and more cities have large covered areas—atriums, elevated tunnels and skyways—that are ideal for walkers. The choices are endless.

If you need a fresh idea, many hotels and community recreation departments will provide you with walking maps that have courses already laid out for you. Are you aware of the proliferation of walking courses planned and maintained by businesses, hospitals, retirement homes, and city recreation departments? Frequently these courses are designed with stopping places where notices are posted describing exercises you might want to take during your walk.

If the report by President Reagan's Commission on Americans Outdoors has any effect, then we may eventually see a system of "greenways," nationwide corridors of open space along rivers and streams, abandoned rail lines, utility rights-of-way, and similar sites in cities and suburbs that will be set aside for walking. The greenways would make grassy walks readily accessible to urbanites and suburbanites who would otherwise probably settle for a sidewalk. It will take a lot of citizen support to make this happen.

To many walkers, gearing up and being outdoors is vital to the pleasure they get from walking. They find the warmth of the sun, the brisk cold of the winter, and communion with nature part of the experience of walking. But striding outdoors is not the only way to get the exercise you need, and for many people it may not be the most enjoyable. What you give up of the poetic beauties of nature, you may make up in comfort by walking indoors. You forgo disagreeable heat or cold as well as unfriendly dogs, uneven walking surfaces, bugs, smog, and other annoyances. When the temperature soars or drops dramatically, seniors and cardiac patients *should* move indoors.

If there is an indoor track near you, you can probably get permission to use it. A track's advantage is that you can easily keep a record of your distance. The disadvantage of a track is that it's boring. Be sure to bring a Walkman or a friend.

Recently, the shopping mall, besides being a place for consumer pleasure, has become an arena for fitness walking. Mall-walking groups have sprung up all over the country, so there is plenty of company out there for anyone interested in mall-walking. Mall owners have responded enthusiastically, opening mall doors early to give the walkers time for their exercise before serious shoppers arrive.

Malls are designed for walking, so why not take advantage of them? They're safe and well lit. There's no traffic. The walking surface is smooth and even. It's never too hot or cold or too rainy or snowy. Mall-walking is particularly good for the elderly and those recovering from illness, because those long corridors offer a safe place to exercise your way back to fitness. We have been recommending mall-walking to people for many years.

A variation of indoor walking is rink-walking. In New England, where winter temperatures sometimes make outdoor walking dangerous, some ice skating rinks are allowing walkers to use the perimeter of the rink for fitness walking. For a small fee you can walk on a premeasured track and have the pleasure of watching the skaters.

More information about walking activities is available through the clubs and organizations listed in the Appendix of this book.

Hiking and Backpacking

If you have been faithful to your fitness-walking program for twenty weeks or more and are looking for a more adventurous way to walk, you may want to take a day hike. There are thousands of miles of hiking trails in the United States, and almost every state and local recreation department can give you maps of trails in your area. Both the Appalachian Mountain Club and the Sierra Club publish excellent guidebooks to trails in all regions of the country.

If you are interested in hiking, be prepared for a very different kind of walking.

Taking a hike is an adventure. There are new things to see around every bend, at the top of every hill, and at the bottom of every ravine. There's a pond, a strange bird, a new mountain view—the variety is endless, the view is never the same. Most important, in hiking you have a goal, some place you want to get to, whether it is the top of a hill or a fishing stream or a campsite.

Hiking is a challenge. The footing varies from slippery to steep to smooth and flat. You may be wading a stream one hour and climbing a cliff the next. To cope with some of these challenges, you need to equip yourself with a guidebook for day hiking that includes topographical maps of hiking trails. The Geological Survey Maps are excellent, though reading a topographical map is a skill in itself. Once you learn what the lines on the maps mean, you will be prepared when the elevation of your trail rises steeply and you will know which branch to take when your trail forks. Hikers compare the sense of independence gained from knowing how to follow such a map to the pleasure an explorer feels when he first enters a new territory.

Here are some tips from experienced hikers:

• Adopt a comfortable pace and a relatively slow stride. With hiking you are in for the long haul, and walking fast over strange terrain is very tiring. This is not a competition. No one is going to speed by you with a number on his chest.

• Study your topographical map and figure out the elevations of the trail you are hiking before you leave; then make adjustments in how far you plan to hike. The rule of thumb is that every 1,000 feet of elevation is equal to one mile of hiking on flat ground.

• If selecting shoes for fitness walking deserves attention, selecting boots for hiking requires some careful research. You may need shoes with a special sole that clings to rocks and other uneven surfaces. The best sole is made of Vibram. Get the lightest pair of shoes possible for the weight you will be carrying. Every pound on your feet is equal to five pounds on your back, and shoes vary in weight from two to six pounds. However, if you are backpacking and carrying a lot of weight, the lightest shoe may not be strong enough for you. Many companies that make good walking shoes also make good shoes or boots with special features for hiking.

• Backpacking is an advanced form of day hiking in which you carry food, shelter, and clothing with you on your back. It probably would cost about $300 to outfit yourself with the rudiments of pack, tent, sleeping bag, boots, and other equipment you need for backpacking, but you may want to borrow or rent equipment the first time out. A backpacking trip typically lasts two to seven days and the pack weighs between twenty and thirty pounds. For this kind of exercise you need training. Begin with short hikes, carrying a light pack, and gradually work up until you can carry twenty or thirty pounds for six or seven hours.

• A day's hike for an experienced hiker with a pack lasts between six and eight hours and covers between eight and twelve miles, depending on terrain. Many hikers like to travel with a group of friends and make the object of their hike a trout stream where they hope to catch their dinner. Others hike to be by themselves.

Several words of caution are in order for hikers and backpackers.

Of course, you are very much at the mercy of the weather. Rain can come up unexpectedly and at higher elevations snow can fall as late as early June or as early as the beginning of October. If you climb from the valley floor where it's warm into the mountains, you need to remember that it gets cold in the evening and even colder if you are spending the night.

Lightning is dangerous, especially at higher elevations. Follow the usual precautions. Don't stand under a tree. Seek shelter if possible. Obviously you should not go out in thunderstorms. Consult the weather service in the area before planning an extensive hike.

Hypothermia occurs more commonly with hikers and backpackers than with other walkers because once they get wet it is difficult for them to get warm and dry. If you fall in a stream or get drenched with rain, stop and build a fire or at least dry yourself off before you get chilled.

Listen to your body. Especially if you are hiking alone, heed any persistent pain as a warning sign of trouble. You can't wait to see what will happen, because there is no medical help readily available in case the problem turns into an emergency. The best advice is to look for help at the first sign of trouble.

If you dream of hiking in exotic and primitive places, Lonely Planet travel books will guide you on hikes through

Turkey, Kashmir, Ecuador, and forty other exciting countries. Published by an Australian company, the guides emphasize trekking with cheap accommodations and food. For $10 a year you can subscribe to the newsletter. You can get a free catalogue of guidebooks by writing to Lonely Planet, P.O. Box 2001-A, Berkeley, CA 94702.

Safety

Besides avoiding problems with your feet, ankles, and legs, you need to avoid dangers in your walking environment. Traffic is the chief hazard, so take all the precautions that any pedestrian should take. Walk on sidewalks if possible and be careful at intersections. If you must walk in the street, be sure to face traffic. You need your ears to hear as well as your eyes to see, so don't turn on your Walkman if you're in the street or crossing it.

After dark, you face another problem: You are almost invisible. According to police accounts, in more than 85 percent of the cases in which motorists killed pedestrians, the motorist claimed not to have seen the pedestrian in time to stop. At one time or another, almost all of us have had to slam on the car brakes to avoid hitting a pedestrian. Yet it's hard to remember how invisible we are when we are the pedestrian. Light-colored clothes help but are not enough to prevent accidents. At night you need to wear reflective clothing or tape. This reflects three hundred times more light than a white surface. The best system outlines head, waist, arms, and legs. Since moving parts are more noticeable than still ones, put reflective tape on your shoes—back and front.

Dogs may be man's best friend, but as your mail carrier will tell you, they often look pretty threatening to a person striding into the dog's territory. Do not run. Saying "Go home!" to the dog in a loud and commanding voice is often all you need to do. A rain of small stones may drive him away.

Or you can carry one of the various dog repellent sprays or noisemakers that are available.

Finally, of course, avoid dark streets and dangerous neighborhoods. If you do inadvertently enter a menacing area, stay alert, avoid dark alleyways and doorways, and don't hesitate to run or call for help if you feel threatened.

5

SPECIAL CONCERNS

Pregnancy

Even in the days when polite society referred to pregnancy as "a delicate condition" and thought pregnant women should stay at home with their feet up, doctors considered walking to be good exercise for expectant mothers. Now that many pregnant women are putting in a full day's work, doctors haven't changed their minds.

Though pregnancy is not the time for a normally sedentary woman to begin a vigorous fitness program, you can safely start walking for exercise. Walking helps control weight, raises spirits, and enhances appearance. Walking maintains fitness without the fatigue and the stress on joints and tendons that running causes in a pregnant woman.

The changes that take place in a woman's body during pregnancy make walking an especially appropriate exercise for you during that time:

• Changes in hormone levels may cause connective tissue and ligaments to loosen slightly, making joints more susceptible to injury. Walking avoids the bouncing of jogging and the jerky movements of tennis, both of which can be uncomfortable during pregnancy.

• As the uterus increases in size, lung space is reduced and there is less room for the increased oxygen reserve needed for aerobic exercises. A pregnant woman should moderate her activity to avoid becoming too short of breath. A good way to assess this is to use "perceived exertion" as your guide to walking speed. Exert yourself slightly less during pregnancy than you did before. Slow down even more during the second and third trimesters.

• As the uterus grows, it causes the spine to arch, which affects posture and sense of balance. Walking does not demand the same degree of balance needed by aerobic dance or even jogging. It also helps build gluteal muscles and stretch paraspinal muscles to relieve or prevent the back pain often associated with an arched spine.

• Increasing strain on the sacroiliac, hip joints, and back, as well as swelling of the legs and ankles, can cause balance problems. Walking improves circulation, which may moderate the swelling.

• While walking does not replace the leg elevation recommended for varicose veins, it may in some cases augment that treatment.

While walking is healthful, getting overheated may be hazardous for your baby. The American College of Obstetricians and Gynecologists recommends that a pregnant woman never exercise when she has a fever or when it is hot and humid outside. She should keep her exercise heart rate at 140 beats per minute or lower, and her internal temperature under 100.4 degrees F. She should avoid dehydration by drinking four to eight ounces of cool water for every ten or fifteen minutes of exercise in warm weather.

Sedentary women should begin slowly with a pace of two miles per hour for twenty minutes, and then gradually work up to three or four miles per hour for thirty minutes. More active pregnant women should not exceed fifteen minutes of strenuous exercise at a time; they should feel good after exercise and not feel any pain or discomfort. Remember to allow plenty of time to warm up and cool down and obey the maximum-140-beats-per-minute rule. If you develop leg cramps, uterine cramps, shortness of breath, pain, or any unusual symptoms, stop walking and consult your doctor.

You should ask your doctor to help select a walking plan to suit your special needs. You should check with him or her, too, about returning to your usual fitness-walking program after the baby is born.

Injury Rehabilitation

Whenever a cast is removed from a broken leg, it is obvious the leg muscles have atrophied; they are smaller and weaker than before they were immobilized. This dramatically illustrates what happens to muscles that are not used for any length of time. In a famous Swedish study, five healthy medical students confined to bed for twenty-one days lost an astonishing 27 percent of their cardiovascular fitness.

Walking helps muscles recover from atrophy due to inactivity, and it helps a person regain cardiovascular fitness. For upper-body injuries, walking supports conditioning while the body heals. Patients with knee or ankle injuries won't begin their rehabilitation with walking, but in a later stage of recovery walking becomes an excellent way to ease back into regular activities.

Getting patients out of bed and walking after surgery helps prevent serious complications like blood clots in the legs or the lungs, urinary tract infections, and slowing of the bowel. These complications impede recovery and can themselves be life-threatening. Patients can be on their feet shuffling slowly down the hall less than twenty-four hours after many operations.

When you become sick or injured, talk to your doctor about returning to your walking program. He or she can give you good advice about the best way for you to return to your normal level of physical activity.

Cardiac Rehabilitation

At the University of Massachusetts Medical Center, as in many hospitals, walking is a cornerstone in our rehabilitation of heart-attack patients. The "training effect" of exercise—an increase in maximum oxygen consumption and a decrease in heart rate, among other things, occur in people with heart disease after six to eight weeks of exercise, just as they do in everybody else. This improvement hastens heart patients' return to normal activities, while also helping them to avoid another heart attack.

Our program for cardiac rehabilitation has four phases. The exercise portion of the first phase of the program involves having a patient reach the level of climbing one flight of stairs or walking 500 feet on a level hallway without showing symptoms. This must occur before the patient can be discharged from the hospital. The patient begins by moving with assistance and progresses to increasingly vigorous activity. Seven to ten days after the attack and before leaving the hospital, we give a patient a low-level exercise tolerance test on the treadmill and a progressive prescription for walking.

In Phase 2 a patient returns to the hospital for weekly exercise classes where we monitor his or her physical condition. During this phase patients exercise to increase their heart rates to a maximum of 60 percent of the rate achieved on their low-level exercise tolerance test. This phase of the program also includes education about controlling risk factors connected with eating, smoking, and drinking.

By Phase 3 a patient usually has returned to work. We schedule exercise classes three times a week until a patient achieves his or her training goals, usually about 75 percent of maximum heart rate, sustained for fifteen to twenty minutes during each session. We teach patients to monitor their own pulse rate and to stop exercising if symptoms occur. This phase, which continues to emphasize reducing all risk factors, usually continues for three or four months.

Finally, we refer our patients to a local exercise program which operates with advice from members of the hospital staff. Patients are tested once or twice a year to assess their progress and update their exercise prescriptions.

Besides reducing the likelihood of a second heart attack and improving patients' strength and endurance, our exercise program reduces the patients' sense of helplessness, increases their self-confidence, and returns to them some of the control over their lives and bodies that the heart attack took away. It is very important to recognize, however, that for cardiac patients, just like everyone else, walking by itself is not enough. Our walking program is combined with risk-factor reduction to lower cholesterol and control blood pressure. No adult, whether or not he or she has heart disease, should smoke cigarettes!

Two patients' stories help illustrate important points about exercise and cardiac rehabilitation. A successful thirty-year-old man named Jeff came to the clinic with what seemed to be a chronic cold that left him short of breath even when he was resting. Examination revealed that he had congestive heart failure, a serious condition very unusual in such a young person. After Jeff got over his initial shock and the depression of learning how dangerously sick he was, he asked for a progressive walking program. Initially Jeff was so weak that he walked less that a quarter of a mile. But his determination never flagged and he kept going. A year later Jeff was walking four miles a day, avoiding salt, and monitoring his blood pressure and cholesterol. While Jeff's heart is only minimally stronger, his muscles are so much more efficient that he can work a normal day without being short of breath. Walking helped Jeff reclaim his life.

Another patient, a man in his fifties named Grant, had had a heart attack four years before he was referred to us. Grant had made all the right changes in his life: He stopped smoking, lost weight, and became a serious jogger. Then, suddenly, Grant began feeling lightheaded while jogging. He went to his family doctor, who diagnosed him as having dangerous extra heartbeats and referred him to our medical center. After running some tests, we told Grant he needed to come into the hospital and to get on medications to control his heart rhythm. He refused, saying hospitals and doctors hadn't done him any good. The original success of his running program convinced Grant he could care for himself without medical help. Two weeks later Grant died while jogging, from a condition we could have treated.

If you have cardiac disease, it is unrealistic and dangerous to expect that the changes you make in your own life will eliminate the need for medical help. Be sensible: Control the risk factors in your life with the help of your physician. Sometimes that means taking tests and medications as well as walking.

Diabetes

Walking is excellent exercise for diabetics. By increasing the body's sensitivity to insulin and lowering blood-sugar levels, walking helps decrease the amount of insulin that many diabetics need. Walking helps control obesity, a problem often associated with diabetes, and reduces the likelihood of cardiovascular disease, the leading cause of death among diabetics. At the same time, walking does not put too much strain on the cardiovascular system or on the diabetic's muscles and joints, which may be fragile.

Diabetics must be careful, however. They should carry a

piece of candy to ward off hypoglycemia (low blood sugar), bring identification that says they are diabetic, and either take along a companion or be sure someone knows when and where they plan to walk.

A diabetic's feet are especially vulnerable to infection because blood vessels and nerves in this area often become impaired. A common blister can become a serious problem, since poor circulation does not readily allow antibiotics to reach the infected spot on the diabetic's foot. Since a diabetic may feel little pain in his or her feet, a blister can get out of hand before it is noticeable. To avoid this condition, diabetics should wash their feet and examine them for injuries after every walk. Properly fitted shoes and clean, dry, absorbent socks are doubly important. If questions about foot care arise, consult a podiatrist. We recommend that all diabetics who are starting a fitness-walking program first consult with a podiatrist to ensure that their feet are in optimum condition and to minimize the chance of blisters or other problems.

Other Medical Concerns

Walking is an important component in the treatment of several other medical conditions. Chronic obstructive pulmonary disease, a condition usually caused by smoking cigarettes, seriously impairs the victim's capacity to walk and move around. While most patients' capacity for activity remains limited, many improve if they faithfully follow a walking program. Consult with a local pulmonary (lung) physician if you have this problem but want to start a walking program.

After getting proper medical treatment, people with arthritis often find that a medically supervised walking program helps them keep active.

In peripheral vascular disease, which is a narrowing of the arteries supplying the limbs, patients sometimes get a pain in the muscles of their legs. After seeing a physician, patients often improve through a progressive walking program.

Walking can play a major role in reducing hypertension and cholesterol and in controlling obesity and osteoporosis. These conditions are discussed elsewhere in this book.

6

TECHNIQUES

O ne of the greatest aspects of fitness walking is its simplicity. We need to resist the temptation to take this inherently simple, pleasurable activity and make it too complicated. However, there are a few areas where attention to technique can make your walk even more enjoyable and safer.

Stride

To reap all the physical and mental benefits from walking, begin with good posture. Shoulders should be back but relaxed, chest out, eyes ahead, and chin up. To maximize fitness gains and make your walking a total body activity, swing your arms in a natural rhythm with your stride. Our tests show that people naturally adjust the length of their stride according to how fast they want to walk. Forcing yourself to lengthen or shorten your stride makes your walk much less efficient.

How do you discover your best stride length? Simply stand with your feet together and slowly begin to lean forward at the ankles (not the waist). As your weight falls forward, put your foot out and catch yourself. That is your natural stride length.

There are three basic walking strides: strolling at approximately three miles per hour or more with arms swinging loosely at the sides; brisk fitness walking at approximately four miles per hour with an energetic arm motion; and race walking at approximately five miles per hour or more with arms pumping quickly across the chest.

The walking stride is a cycle, with one foot starting halfway through the other's cycle. While one foot swings forward, the other foot supports the body's weight, beginning at the heel and gradually rolling the weight forward along the outer edge of the sole to the ball of the foot and finally to the big toe for the push-off. Before the push-off, the heel of the other foot has struck the ground at about a 45-degree angle and is ready to accept the weight as the first foot begins its swing.

The calf muscles of the legs are the most important muscles in walking. They generate 80 percent of your forward motion. At the push-off, the most energy-demanding part of the stride, the calf muscles shorten to accelerate and push the body forward.

You can trust your body to match the length of your stride to the speed you want, and you can also trust it to choose walking or running, depending on how fast you want to travel. Most people find walking more efficient than running if they want to travel at four miles per hour. At somewhere between four and five miles per hour, for most people the body finds it more efficient to run.

One question we are asked constantly is, Which burns more calories, walking or running? To answer this, it is best to compare the average speed that a person wants to walk with the average speed that a person wants to run. At the speed most people choose for running or walking, running burns up about 20 percent more calories per mile than walking because, though you cover the same horizontal distance, in running you also cover vertical distance; energy is consumed every time a runner propels himself up off the ground. If, on the other hand, you force yourself to walk when your body wants to run, for example, at speeds greater than five miles per hour, you can actually burn more calories walking than running because your motion is much less efficient. By the same token, if you run at speeds less than four miles per hour, you will burn many more calories than you would walking, because at this slow speed, your body would prefer to be walking and running is very inefficient.

Race Walking

At first sight the race walker's wiggling hips and rolling gait may make you smile, but don't be fooled. Race walkers are first-class athletes—the best can walk faster than most people can run. Many are national heroes, particularly in Mexico, which has produced several Olympic race-walking champions. Like soccer and bicycle racing, race walking is gradually catching on in the United States.

As a race walker pushes himself to walk faster than five miles an hour, his body realizes it is much more efficient for him to run than to walk. To walk as efficiently as possible at speeds greater than six miles per hour, race walkers adopt special techniques very different from the stride we use for regular fitness walking. Though few walkers aim to become race walkers, learning their basic technique may give you some insight into your own stride and help you increase your speed.

The race-walking techniques that make you smile are really adaptations of fitness-walking techniques that allow race walkers to take longer strides faster. Like fitness walkers, race walkers use their arms as fulcrums to drive them forward.

The stride is basically the same as the fitness-walking stride. Don't rush to quicken your pace. Speed will come as you learn the technique.

The upper body should be straight but should lean forward slightly. Avoid bending at the waist.

Use the natural swing of the arms but bend them at a 90-degree angle at the elbow and hold them comfortably close to your body for increased momentum and balance. Move them across your chest but no higher than your chest. The motion will be quick and jerky.

The hip movement of race walking is very different from that of fitness walking. It is this distinctive motion that lengthens the race walker's stride and thrusts him forward. The key to fast race walking lies in developing flexible hip action. The movement rotates from front to back with little swing from side to side. Shoulders and hips should move proportionately.

The forward leg swings out and the foot lands well back on the heel, with the toe up. The straightened leg, with the calf muscle relaxed, pulls back to complement the rotating action of the hip. This motion smooths and speeds the forward progress.

As the leg follows through with the pulling action, the weight of your body rolls off the foot onto the toes. As the leg leaves the ground and swings forward, it bends at the knee to just skim over the ground as it moves on its way forward. Each step should land directly in front of the other on a straight line.

The whole body—feet, legs, hips, shoulders, arms, and torso—all must be coordinated to give the walker the proper style, the source of the racer's speed. The heel-to-toe action creates forward momentum, the legs thrust the body forward, the hips rotate to lengthen the stride, and the short, quick arm swing adds power and balance. Race walking gives the total body an excellent workout, which may be why many race walkers begin the sport in middle age.

There are two main rules in formal race walking. First, you must have one foot on the ground at all times. As you walk, make sure your front foot is on the ground before you lift the rear one. If both feet are off the ground at once, you are running, not walking. Second, the knee of the leg that is under you supporting your body must be straight momentarily. In fitness walking, as in running, this knee is bent. This straightening of the knee is what makes your hips wiggle.

All this may be difficult and funny-looking at first, but once the motion is smooth and flowing, it does not feel at all awkward and you may get the urge to try it more often. If you are thinking about race walking, the best advice is to get a coach or join a club so that you can get instruction in proper technique. There are 2,000 competitive and about 10,000 noncompetitive race walkers in the United States. You may want to join them. To learn more, contact Sal Corello, Racewalking Chairman, The Athletics Congress (TAC), 3466 Roberts Lane N, Arlington, VA 22207. Send a stamped, self-addressed envelope.

Weights

A controversy rages over whether or not to add weights to your hands, legs, or torso when you walk. Advocates say that weights help burn calories and increase upper-body strength.

At our Exercise Physiology and Nutrition Laboratory, we conducted experiments in which men and women carried weights totaling 10 percent to 40 percent of their body weight on their trunk while walking three or four miles per hour. Although we found that the increased load led to a significantly greater expenditure of energy, we concluded, Why complicate something that is so easy? We learned that it is uncomfortable to walk with weights and that it is preferable for your total fitness simply to walk faster. Just because a few people want to increase the intensity of the exercise doesn't make walking with weights the next logical step for the average person.

Here are some other points to consider before you load yourself with weights during your next walk:

• Carrying hand weights while walking raises your blood pressure. Although not of concern to the average person, the increase for those with high blood pressure could be dangerous.

• Weighting the extremities increases the likelihood of joint injury. In walking, the left arm balances the right leg and vice versa. The whole body is involved in the walking motion. If you weigh down those extremities, you throw off the delicate balance between arms and legs. Carrying extra weights in your hands might be acceptable for some advanced fitness walkers who want to build upper-body strength, but that is not the aim of a typical fitness-walking program. Leg weights are virtually always contraindicated because they can cause serious damage to hips, knees, and ankles.

• Carrying weights may improve muscle strength while you walk, but this combination of weight-swinging and walking may not be as effective as adding high-repetition, low-weight training as a separate component of your overall fitness program if your goal is to build upper-body strength.

• Whether or not the addition of weights "improves" walking as an exercise, the fact is that we know that walking alone promotes health if it is done as a consistent, life-long activity. That is not to be confused with a short-term program to improve conditioning; both goals are important, but the means to achieve them may be quite different.

• Carrying weights on the trunk or extremities helps in weight loss because you increase the work you perform while walking. Walking without weights is more pleasant, however, and it is an excellent adjunct to a weight-loss program. The point is, when people find an activity enjoyable, they are likely to stick with it for an extended period of time.

7

NUTRITION

A Balanced Diet

Let's be blunt: Diet plays a role in almost all major health problems in America—heart disease, cancer, obesity, elevated cholesterol, and high blood pressure. Unfortunately, because of bizarre notions like the grapefruit diet and some of the nutritionally unbalanced liquid diets, many people have lost sight of the real principles of good eating. In fact, the best diet rests on the simple ideas of variety, moderation, and balance and includes foods with fats, carbohydrates, fiber, and protein. A good diet can easily be adjusted to fit almost anybody's nutritional needs—including the fitness walker's—whether the person is young or old, pregnant or breastfeeding, with or without health problems.

Most Americans' diets are not balanced and moderate. The American Heart Association (AHA) and the Surgeon General's Report on Nutrition have concluded that Americans eat too much fat, salt, and alcohol, and too little carbohydrates and fiber. This imbalance increases the risk of getting almost every one of the life-threatening diseases, especially cardiovascular disease. The American Heart Association has designed a diet that corrects this imbalance and provides satisfying low-calorie foods for overweight people. We have written a book entitled *The Rockport Walking Program* (Prentice Hall, 1989), which contains a diet program and recipes which follow all the principles of the AHA diet.

Make the AHA dietary changes over a period of several months so they are integrated into a healthy lifestyle. Don't decide to "go on a diet" for two weeks; learn healthy eating habits you can live with permanently. While the diet includes many specific recommendations, see what works for you and what you can stick with for a long time.

The AHA's nutrition plan outlines a wholesome diet for a healthy, active life. It helps you:

• Meet your daily needs for protein, vitamins, minerals, and other nutrients
• Achieve and maintain your desirable weight
• Reduce your total fat intake to about 30 percent of calories, instead of the typical 37 to 40 percent
• Limit intake of saturated fat to less than 10 percent of total daily calories and cholesterol to less than 300 milligrams per day
• Substitute polyunsaturated fat or monounsaturated fat for saturated fat wherever possible and don't eat too much of any kind of fat
• Limit your intake of meat, seafood, and poultry to no more than five to seven ounces per day
• Use chicken or turkey without skin or fish in most of your main meals
• Choose lean cuts of meat, trim visible fat, and throw away the fat that cooks out of the meat
• Substitute meatless or low-meat dishes for regular entrees

• Use no more than a total of five to eight teaspoons of fats and oils per day for cooking, baking, and salads
• Consume low-fat dairy products
• Lower cholesterol by using no more than two egg yolks a week (including those used in cooking) and limiting your consumption of organ meats

The AHA diet* is outlined below. This eating plan can help you start a new lifestyle.

◆

VEGETABLES AND FRUITS

High in vitamins, minerals, potassium, fiber; low in fat, calories, sodium. Contain *no* cholesterol.

OKAY FOODS:

Almost all vegetables and fruits are "Okay Foods" and should be part of your daily eating plan.

Use at least three servings (Sv) of fruit or real fruit juice every day (1 Sv = 1 medium-sized piece of fruit or ½ cup juice or canned fruit). Also, use at least three servings of vegetables every day (1 Sv = ½ to 1 cup, cooked or raw).

Include *at least one serving* from the "High Vitamin C" list every day and *at least one serving* from the "High Vitamin A" list several times a week.

HIGH VITAMIN C—asparagus, broccoli, cabbage, cantaloupe, grapefruit, greens (mustard, beet, kale, collards), green pepper, oranges, potatoes, spinach, strawberries, tangerines, tomatoes.

---

*Reproduced with permission. "The American Heart Association Diet, An Eating Plan for Healthy Americans," Dallas, Texas, 1985.

HIGH VITAMIN A—broccoli, cantaloupe, carrots, greens, peaches, pumpkin, spinach, sweet potatoes, winter squash.

When you are reducing your intake of red meat and egg yolks, you can *increase your iron intake* by eating more green, leafy vegetables; peas and beans (fresh and dried); dried fruits; and whole-grain or enriched cereals. *Your body can make better use of the iron these foods provide if you eat them along with a good source of Vitamin C.*

Enjoy plenty of vegetables and fruits. If you are watching your weight, these foods will give you the most nutrition for the fewest calories.

FOODS TO AVOID:

Almost all fruits and vegetables are very low in fat, except:

COCONUT OIL, PALM OIL, AND PALM KERNEL OIL—contain saturated fat and should be avoided.

OLIVES▲* AND AVOCADOS—also contain fat (and therefore are higher in calories). Tips for using these are included in the "Fats and Oils" section.

---

*BE SALT WISE:

The following codes used in the food lists identify store-bought foods that are usually very high in salt or fat.

- ▲ means that although the food is okay for occasional use, it has a high salt content that cannot be removed.
- ● means the food usually contains salt, but good low-salt products are available.
- ■ means the food is high in both salt and dietary fat and cholesterol, making it a very poor food choice.

♦

MILK PRODUCTS

High in protein, calcium, phosphorus, niacin, riboflavin, vitamins A and D

OKAY FOODS:

MILK PRODUCTS CONTAINING ONLY 0–1 PERCENT MILK FAT—skim milk or fluid nonfat milk (0 percent fat); low-fat milk (1 percent fat); nonfat or low-fat dry milk; evaporated skim milk; buttermilk made from skim or low-fat milk; skim or low-fat yogurt; drinks made with skim or low-fat milk and cocoa or other low-fat drink powders; ice milk, sherbet, frozen low-fat yogurt.

LOW-FAT CHEESES—dry-curd or low-fat cottage cheese▲; low-fat natural cheeses▲ or processed special cheeses▲ *labeled as containing not more than 2 grams of fat per ounce.*

Begin trying milk products that are lower in fat. Whole milk is 4 percent fat. If you use whole milk now, first try 2 percent fat milk . . . Then move along to 1 percent fat milk. . . . Soon, you will enjoy the taste of skim milk.

Look for milk products labeled *fortified with vitamins A and D.* Adults and young children need two servings daily (1 Sv = 8 oz. low-fat or skim milk or yogurt, 2 oz. low-fat cheese, of ⅓ cup low-fat cottage cheese); older children, teenagers, and women who are pregnant or breast-feeding need three to four servings.

FOODS TO AVOID:

MILK CONTAINING MORE THAN 1 PERCENT MILK FAT—low-fat milk with 1½ to 2 percent milk fat; whole milk; dried whole milk; buttermilk or yogurt made from whole milk; drinks made from whole milk; condensed milk; evaporated milk; ice cream.

CREAM, ALL KINDS—half and half, heavy, whipping, or sour.

NONDAIRY CREAM SUBSTITUTES—coffee creamers, sour cream substitutes made with coconut, palm, or palm kernel oil, which are high in saturated fat. Look for special ones labeled *made from polyunsaturated fat*.

ALL CHEESES CONTAINING MORE THAN 2 GRAMS OF FAT PER OUNCE—cream cheese■, creamed cottage cheese■, and most other natural and processed cheeses■ such as American, Swiss, mozzarella, and bleu.

---◆---

BREADS, CEREALS, PASTA, AND STARCHY VEGETABLES

Low in fat and cholesterol; high in B vitamins, iron, fiber

OKAY FOODS:

LOW-FAT BREADS—all kinds (wheat, rye, raisin, white); those with whole-grain or enriched flours are best. (1 Sv = 1 slice)

LOW-FAT ROLLS—English muffins, frankfurter and hamburger buns, water (not egg) bagels, pita bread, tortillas (not fried).

LOW-FAT CRACKERS AND SNACKS—animal, graham, rye saltine●, oyster●, and matzo crackers; store-bought fig bar, ginger snap, and molasses cookies; bread sticks, melba toast, rusks, and flatbread; pretzels●, popcorn● (with "Okay" fat).

Hᴏᴛ ᴏʀ Cᴏʟᴅ Cᴇʀᴇᴀʟs—all kinds, except granola-type cereals with coconut or coconut oil (1 Sv = ¼ to ¾ cup).

Rɪᴄᴇ ᴀɴᴅ Pᴀsᴛᴀ—all kinds, except pasta made with egg (1 Sv = ½ cup).

Sᴛᴀʀᴄʜʏ Vᴇɢᴇᴛᴀʙʟᴇs—potatoes, lima beans, green peas, winter squash, corn, yams, or sweet potatoes (1 Sv = ¼ to ¾ cup).

Quɪᴄᴋ Bʀᴇᴀᴅs—home-made with "Okay" fats, oils, and milk products: biscuits, muffins, cornbread, banana bread, soft rolls, pancakes, French toast, and waffles. Use your weekly egg allowance (2 per week), or try egg whites in recipes. Use two egg whites instead of one whole egg.

Lᴏw-Fᴀᴛ Sᴏᴜᴘs—broth●, boullion●, chicken noodle●, tomato-based seafood chowders●, minestrone●, onion●, split pea●, tomato●, vegetarian vegetable●. Use the canned or powdered varieties, but read labels to choose those lowest in salt and fat. Better still, make soups at home so that you can avoid salt, fat, cream, whole milk, or cheese (1 Sv = 1 cup).

Breads, cereals, pasta, and starchy vegetables (in moderate-size portions) are not extremely high in calories. It's the fat and sauces added to them that run up the total calories.

Stretch your meat allowance and your budget by combining small portions of poultry, fish, or meat with vegetables, herbs, and rice or pasta.

FOODS TO AVOID:

PRODUCTS MADE WITH EGG YOLKS OR WITH "AVOID" FATS, OILS, AND WHOLE MILK PRODUCTS. These include any of the following:

Butter rolls, egg breads, egg bagels, cheese breads, croissants, commercial doughnuts, muffins, sweet rolls, biscuits, waffles, pancakes; buttered popcorn■; store-bought mixes.

High-fat commercial crackers such as cheese crackers■, butter crackers■, and those made with coconut or palm oil.

Pasta, rice, and vegetables prepared with whole eggs, cream sauce, or high-fat cheese; or fried in "Avoid" fats.

Cream soups■, vichysoisse■, and chunky-style soups■ that have large amounts of meat in them.

---♦---

MEAT, POULTRY, SEAFOOD, NUTS, DRIED BEANS, PEAS, AND EGGS

High in protein, B vitamins, iron, other minerals.

OKAY FOODS:

CHICKEN AND TURKEY—trim the skin; this is where much of the fat is found.

LEAN BEEF, VEAL, PORK, LAMB—trim all visible fat.

FISH AND SHELLFISH—all kinds, but limit the use of shrimp or lobster to *no more than* one serving of one of these per week.

Meatless or "Low-Meat" Main Dishes—try recipes with dried beans, peas, lentils, soybean curd (tofu), peanut butter●, or low-fat cheese▲ instead of meat a few times a week. Also try combining small amounts of meat, fish, or poultry with rice or pasta in mixed dishes or casseroles.

Egg Whites—but limit whole eggs or egg yolks to no more than three per week.

Wild Game—rabbit, pheasant, venison, wild duck, and other wild game animals generally have less fat than animals raised for the market.

Adults need no more than 6 ounces of meat, poultry, or seafood per day (about two small servings). Examples of a 3-ounce portion:

> ½ of a chicken breast or a chicken leg and a thigh together
> ½ cup of flaked fish
> 2 thin slices lean roast beef ($3'' \times 3'' \times \frac{1}{4}''$)

Preschool children should have about 1 ounce of meat, poultry, or seafood per day for each year of age.

Use poultry (without the skin) and fish more often than red meat.

Instead of high-fat luncheon meats, choose low-fat processed sandwich meats with *labels showing no more than 2 grams fat per ounce,* such as turkey▲ or chicken roll▲, turkey ham▲, turkey pastrami▲, or lean boiled ham▲.

Buy only the leanest ground beef, *labeled as containing no more than 15 percent fat.* Pour off the fat after browning. Ask your butcher for the fat content if it is not noted on the label.

Skim the fat off meat juices before adding to stews, soups, and gravies. Chilling the meat juices first allows you to easily remove the hardened fat.

FOODS TO AVOID:

MEATS—"prime" grade and other heavily marbled and fatty meats such as corned beef■, regular pastrami■, short ribs, spare ribs, rib eye roast or steak, regular ground meat, frankfurters■, sausage■, bacon■, and high-fat luncheon meats■.

GOOSE AND DOMESTIC DUCK—too fatty.

ORGAN MEATS—brains, chitterlings, gizzard, heart, kidney, sweetbreads, pork maws, and liver are high in cholesterol. However, liver is so rich in iron and vitamins that a small serving (3 ounces) is recommended about once a month.

FATS AND OILS

Some of these foods are high in Vitamins A or E, but *all* are high in fat and calories. The amount of food per serving (Sv) is described for each item so you can keep track of fat intake in teaspoons (tsp).

OKAY FOODS:

VEGETABLE OILS—safflower, sunflower, corn, partially hydro-genated soybean, cottonseed, sesame, canola, olive oils (1 Sv = 1 tsp).

MARGARINES—stick, tub, squeeze (1 Sv = 1 tsp), or diet (1 Sv = 2 tsp). One of the "Okay" vegetable oils should be listed as the first ingredient on the label with twice as much polyunsaturated as saturated fat.

SALAD DRESSING AND MAYONNAISE●—homemade or store-bought, made with "Okay" oils (1 Sv = 2 tsp); low-calorie dressings● can be used as desired.

SEEDS AND NUTS—all seeds● (pumpkin, sesame, sunflower) and most nuts● (except cashew and macadamia) (1 Sv = 3 tsp).

AVOCADOS AND OLIVES▲—use only in small amounts (1 Sv = 3 tsp chopped).

PEANUT BUTTER●—count as a fat (1 Sv = 2 tsp) or use as a "Meatless Main Dish" (1 Sv = 3 tsp).

PEANUT OIL—this choice is not as good as the "Okay" oils; it may be used sparingly for a flavor change (1 Sv = 1 tsp).

Depending upon your need for weight control, use no more than five to eight servings of "Okay" fats and oils per day.

Remember to count the "hidden fats" (in bakery products and snack foods, in cooking, on vegetables and breads).

Use cooking styles that call for little or no fat—instead of frying, try roasting, broiling, steaming.

<u>FOODS TO AVOID:</u>

SOLID FATS AND SHORTENINGS—butter●, bacon drippings■, ham hocks■, lard, salt pork■, meat fat and drippings, gravy from meat drippings, shortening, suet; margarines except those listed as "Okay."

CHOCOLATE, COCONUT, COCONUT OIL, PALM OIL, OR PALM KERNEL OIL—these are often used in bakery products, nondairy creamers, whipped toppings, candy, and commercially fried foods. *Read labels carefully.*

DESSERTS, BEVERAGES, AND SNACKS

<u>OKAY FOODS:</u>

The foods listed here are low in saturated fat and cholesterol, but many are high in calories and low in nutritional value. Use the foods from the other five food lists to make your eating plan. Then occasionally choose a few of the foods listed below to add interest. For weight control, select from the first two lists. If you are at your recommended weight, add selections from the "Other Choices" list (below).

FIRST CHOICE (low in calories or no calories)—raw vegetables, fresh fruit, fruit canned without sugar, plain gelatin, tea, coffee, and cocoa powder.

SECOND CHOICE (low in saturated fat, fairly low in calories)— frozen or canned fruit with sugar, dried fruits, seeds, "Okay" nuts●, plain popcorn●, pretzels●, "Okay" crackers● or cookies, sherbet, ice milk, frozen or fruited low-fat yogurt, angel food cake.

OTHER CHOICES (HIGHER IN CALORIES):

Foods that are low in fat, also low in nutrition—hard candy, gum drops, flavored gelatin, water ices, fruit punches, carbonated drinks, sugar, syrup, honey, jam, jelly, marmalade.

Special recipe items—homemade desserts (cakes, pies, cookies, and puddings) made with the fats and oils, low-fat milk products, and egg products listed as "Okay."

Alcoholic beverages—if you drink, do so in moderation; no more than two drinks per day of wine, beer, or liquor.

FOODS TO AVOID:

Other desserts and snacks not listed above, such as store-bought cakes, pies, cookies, and mixes; coconut; high-fat snack products such as deep-fried chips■ and rich crackers■; desserts and snacks containing cheese■, cream, or whole milk; and ice cream.

Nutrition and Activity

Although the airwaves and bookstores are full of nutritional information, myriad myths about food and exercise persist. Here are some products you *don't* need to eat if you are physically active: extra protein, extra vitamins and minerals (except for vitamin B), salt tablets, "activity" drinks, extra sugar. The two things you *do* require are carbohydrates for energy and water to replace what you lose when you exercise. Both are easily added to the AHA Diet.

Walkers don't have to make any great changes in their diets. Race walkers, hikers, and backpackers, on the other hand, need a plan for replacing water and energy. The best idea is portable and healthful food. Here are several handy choices:

• Fresh fruits and vegetables, such as apples, pears, oranges, carrots
• Dried fruits, such as raisins, apricots, figs, trail mix
• Other options: low-fat cheese and crackers, oatmeal cookies, graham cracker squares, peanut butter

Overnight backpackers are always on the lookout for food that is not perishable, not fragile, not heavy to carry, and easy to prepare under primitive conditions. Here are some suggestions:

• High carbohydrate foods like beans, lentils, prebaked potatoes, rice, whole-wheat rolls, or oatmeal
• Vegetables that don't mash easily, like string beans, snow peas, squash, or broccoli
• Fruits that don't mash easily, like apples, pears, oranges, or tangerines
• Low-fat cheese like mozzarella or string cheese

Hydration

Most nutritional advice focuses on food while ignoring the equally pressing problem of hydration. Realize this: People of average weight can go for thirty days without eating, but they can't go without drinking for more than seventy-two hours without dying. In a brisk one-hour walk, fitness walkers easily lose a quart of water through sweating and respiration. At that point they have lost 1 to 2 percent of their body weight in water and their performance level falls significantly.

Few fitness walkers realize how vital hydration is. Essentially, human beings *are* water: Males are 60 to 70 percent water, females 50 to 60 percent. Losing 5 percent of body water causes symptoms of dehydration like dizziness, weakness, and difficulty functioning at all. Losing 15 to 20 percent of body water is often fatal. Normally the average adult loses two and a half to three quarts of water a day through urine, stools, sweat, and respiration, but fitness walking in a hot climate can increase that to four quarts.

Water serves four major functions: It maintains performance levels, it supports the blood pressure, it controls body temperature (water is the body's basic coolant), and it carries away waste products. Because water is crucial to every biological system, doctors advise drinking eight eight-ounce glasses of water a day. It may sound like a lot, but it's not. We hardly notice much of the water we consume. It comes in milk or coffee or other beverages or in food. Lettuce, for example, is 95 percent water. Even bread and potatoes contain a tremendous amount of water. Wherever it comes from, your body requires between two and a quarter and four quarts of water a day. The only question is, Do you want it with or without calories?

Unfortunately, in the United States water's major competition is soda. The average American drinks between four and five hundred cans of soft drinks a year, each one containing between eight and twelve teaspoons of sugar or 150 to 180 calories. That's as many calories as you burn in thirty to forty-five minutes of fitness walking. Though diet sodas provide no calories, scientists don't yet understand the effects of eating large quantities of the sugar substitutes, caffeine, and other chemicals which they contain. Our advice: Have sodas now and again if you enjoy their taste, but drink water most of the time. Water is what your body really needs.

Surprisingly, when you are exercising, you cannot rely on thirst to indicate how much water you need. If you wait to be thirsty, your body can take up to twenty-four hours to replenish water lost on a regular fitness walk. To avoid dehydration, drink an eight-ounce glass of water twenty to thirty minutes before walking and carry enough water to consume four ounces every fifteen to twenty minutes, depending on how hot it is. Within a half-hour after your walk, drink another eight ounces of water. While that sounds like a lot, in fact it is only enough to replenish the water your body is losing.

The longer you walk, the more water you need. If you plan to walk for two to four hours, you need eight to twenty ounces of water before you start and four to six ounces every fifteen minutes. For energy on a long walk, substitute juice for water every third time you stop for a drink. If you plan to walk four to six hours, alternate water and juice.

8

WEIGHT LOSS

According to the National Institutes of Health, the statistics involving overweight people in this country are staggering: About 40 million people in the United States are at least 20 percent overweight. Of these about 28 million have increased risk of diabetes, hypertension, high cholesterol, and coronary artery disease. In fact, of the ten leading causes of death in our country, seven are related to poor nutrition, being overweight, or excessive drinking of alcohol. To these grim statistics we can add the extraordinary preoccupation of our society with a slim, attractive appearance. This is manifest in everything from Jane Fonda video workouts to the bestseller lists to the covers of *Vogue* and *Cosmopolitan.*

In 1988 Surgeon General Koop issued a major report identifying several aspects of the American lifestyle that cause obesity. The Surgeon General's report named major problems in what we eat and the way we live. We eat too much fat, cholesterol, sodium, and alcohol and too little complex carbohydrates and fiber. We are overweight and sedentary. While the changes in diet that the Surgeon General recommended address many serious health problems, for the moment we'd like to focus on how improving your diet helps control your weight and how walking enhances any weight-loss program.

A gram of fat has more than twice the calories found in a gram of protein or carbohydrate, so reducing the fat in our diet has a significant impact on the number of calories we consume. There are nine calories in a gram of fat (and nearly as many in alcohol), compared with only four calories in a gram of carbohydrate or protein. If you want to look as sleek as a Porsche 944, then eat less fat and more carbohydrates and fiber. Another bit of good news: Our patients report that after a time on a low-fat diet, the greasy foods they once found so tempting lost much of their appeal. They may want a slice of pizza, but they don't crave the whole pie.

How Do You Know If You're Overweight?

The problem the public usually identifies as overweight is actually overfat—that is, too large a percentage of weight is fat, too little of it is lean body mass. Women's bodies should be no more than 20 to 25 percent fat; men's bodies no more than 15 to 20 percent fat.

Discovering whether your body is too fat is not as easy as stepping on a scale. In our lab we measure the percentage of the body that is fat by weighing people under water. Because fat floats and lean tissue (muscles, bones, organs, etc.) sinks, we can calculate what percentage of the body is fat (fat weight) and what percentage is lean mass (lean weight) from a person's weight under water. Though this is the best and most accurate test for learning body density, it takes elaborate equipment, a skilled technician, and about an hour to run the test.

There are two tests that are far easier to conduct. One is the "pinch an inch" skinfold or fatfold thickness test, which requires special calipers to measure the thickness of fatfolds at various spots on the body. An equation is used to estimate the percentage of body fat from these measurements. Different skinfold sites and equations are usually used for men and women as well as athletes. Though this test takes practice and training, it gives a fairly accurate measure of total body fat. Staff in exercise and health clubs can make these measurements.

Another measure of body fat is the electrical impedance test, based on the relative conducting power of fat in relation to lean body mass. This test requires a machine that is often available in health clubs, where you can also find people who perform the "pinch an inch" test. Both of these tests take about ten minutes.

For years most people have relied on their bathroom scale and the height and weight tables prepared by the Metropolitan Life Insurance Company—the latest was prepared in 1983—to gauge whether they were overweight (Figure 11). The midpoint of the range is usually used as the desirable weight. On that scale, overweight is defined as 20 percent over standard weight for height and frame; obesity is 40 percent over standard weight for height and frame. Unfortunately, the tables are based simply on the weight of people who lived the longest and have little to do with fat.

A better table is the Body Mass Index (BMI), shown in Figure 12. This is a ratio of weight to height (wt/ht^2). It is not a measure of fat weight, but it does correlate highly with amount of body fat.

The nomogram on page 120 can help facilitate the calculation of BMI. The cut-off points for overweight and obesity are based on large population studies of the health status of Americans. You can also use this nomogram to find your desirable body weight.

All charts, equations, and measurements aside, you need to think carefully about how much you want to weigh. Just as you need to set realistic goals for your walking

FIGURE 11
1983 Metropolitan Height and Weight Tables*

	Men					Women		
Height Feet Inches	Small Frame	Medium Frame	Large Frame		Height Feet Inches	Small Frame	Medium Frame	Large Frame
5 2	128–134	131–141	138–150		4 10	102–111	109–121	118–131
5 3	130–136	133–143	140–153		4 11	103–113	111–123	120–134
5 4	132–138	135–145	142–156		5 0	104–115	113–126	122–137
5 5	134–140	137–148	144–160		5 1	106–118	115–129	125–140
5 6	136–142	139–151	146–164		5 2	108–121	118–132	128–143
5 7	138–145	142–154	149–168		5 3	111–124	121–135	131–147
5 8	140–148	145–157	152–172		5 4	114–127	124–138	134–151
5 9	142–151	148–160	155–176		5 5	117–130	127–141	137–155
5 10	144–154	151–163	158–180		5 6	120–133	130–144	140–159
5 11	146–157	154–166	161–184		5 7	123–136	133–147	143–163
6 0	149–160	157–170	164–188		5 8	126–139	136–150	146–167
6 1	152–164	160–174	168–192		5 9	129–142	139–153	149–170
6 2	155–168	164–178	172–197		5 10	132–145	142–156	152–173
6 3	158–172	167–182	176–202		5 11	135–148	145–159	155–176
6 4	162–176	171–187	181–207		6 0	138–151	148–162	158–179

*Weights at ages 25 to 59 years, based on lowest mortality. Weight in pounds according to frame (in indoor clothing weighing 5 pounds for men and 3 pounds for women; shoes with 1-inch heels).
Source of basic data: 1979 Build Study, Society of Actuaries and Association of Life Insurance Medical Directors of America, 1980.
Courtesy Metropolitan Life Insurance Company.

To make an approximation of your frame size:

Extend your arm and bend the forearm upward at a 90-degree angle. Keep fingers straight and turn the inside of your wrist toward your body. If you have a caliper, use it to measure the space between the two prominent bones on either side of your elbow. Without a caliper, place thumb and index finger of your other hand on these two bones. Measure the space between your fingers against a ruler or tape measure. Compare it with these tables that list elbow measurements for *medium-framed* men and women. Measurements lower than those listed indicate you have a small frame. Higher measurements indicate a large frame.

Men	Height in 1" Heels	Elbow Breadth
	5'2"–5'3"	2 1/2"–2 7/8"
	5'4"–5'7"	2 5/8"–2 7/8"
	5'8"–5'11"	2 3/4"–3"
	6'0"–6'3"	2 3/4"–3 1/8"
	6'4"	2 7/8"–3 1/4"

Women	Height in 1" Heels	Elbow Breadth
	4'10"–4'11"	2 1/4"–2 1/2"
	5'0"–5'3"	2 1/4"–2 1/2"
	5'4"–5'7"	2 3/8"–2 5/8"
	5'8"–5'11"	2 3/8"–2 5/8"
	6'0"	2 1/2"–2 3/4"

Courtesy the Metropolitan Life Insurance Company

119

FIGURE 12

Nomogram for Determining Body Mass Index (BMI)

To use this nomogram, place a ruler or other straight edge between the column for height and the column for weight connecting an individual's numbers for those two variables. Read the BMI in kg/m² where the straight line crosses the middle lines when the height and weight are connected. Overweight: BMI of 25–30 kg/m²; obesity: BMI above 30 kg/m². Heights and weights are without shoes or clothes.

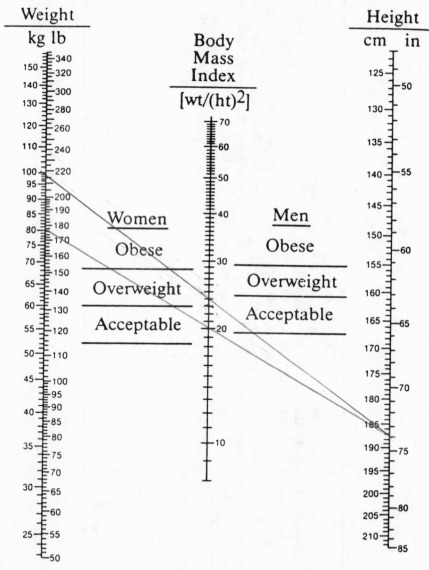

Source: From *The Surgeon General's Report on Nutrition and Health*, U.S. Department of Health and Human Services, Public Health Service, DHH Publication No. 88-50210, Washington, DC.

program, so must you set realistic goals for your weight-loss program. Most people are not naturally built like the models we see on television and in magazines. Target a weight that will make you healthy and happy, but—equally important— aim for a weight you can maintain without feeling half starved all the time.

The Physiology of Exercise and Weight Loss

The way fat accumulates can be described very simply: When you eat more calories than you burn up, the surplus is stored as fat. There are two ways to attack this problem: by consuming fewer calories, by burning more. Though we have become a nation of on-again off-again dieters, studies increasingly show that the true culprit is more often inactivity than excess food intake. Overall the number of calories consumed in the United States has declined by 10 percent since 1900, while obesity has almost doubled during that same time. Many studies have shown that, in general, obese people exercise less than people who are not obese.

If eating too many calories is not the sole culprit in obesity, then we must look at the other side of the equation to discover how burning more calories can contribute to improving our weight.

While you are exercising, the amount of energy you expend increases. For example, a person of average size uses 5 calories per minute walking at three and a half miles per hour. In thirty minutes he or she burns 150 calories, in an hour 300 calories. This is a steady and predictable number. If you continue to walk an hour at three and a half miles per hour for four days a week for a year and eat the same amount of food you always do, you will lose fifteen pounds.

However, exercise contributes more to losing weight than this direct expenditure of calories. Exercise also raises the resting metabolic rate (the minimal rate of energy you use when you are at rest), *even after you stop exercising*. Some studies suggest that the resting metabolic rate is about

10 percent higher for four to six hours following exercise. The amount of increase is based on the intensity and duration of the exercise session.

Exercise also helps you overcome one of your body's most frustrating strategems. Just as you are trying to get rid of excess fat, your body takes steps to conserve it. According to the "set point" theory, when you drastically reduce the number of calories you take in, your body thinks there must be a famine and mobilizes to prevent starvation. Automatically, your body protects its supply of stored energy by lowering the rate at which those calories are burned. The resting metabolic rate can decrease by 12 to 29 percent to conserve energy. This occurs when you are resting and when you are working in order to maintain the fat as near as possible to the set point at which your body began to feel starved. The good news is that you can counteract the "set point" by exercising to keep your metabolic rate high. Some studies also suggest that exercising regularly "resets" the set point at a lower level.

One further metabolic complication: If you take in fewer than 1,200 calories a day, you cannot get all the nutrients your body needs. Furthermore, the brain, which needs blood sugar, or glucose, to function rather than fat, will use lean body tissue to provide energy if you cut your caloric intake under 1,200 a day.

Another way in which exercise increases the effectiveness of dieting is by ensuring that the weight you lose is fat and not lean body mass. When you measured your body composition, you found out what percentage of your body is fat and what percentage is lean body mass. Lean body mass keeps you alive and moving by expending energy through metabolism. Exercise changes the composition of your body; it decreases fat and preserves lean body mass. The more lean body mass you have, the more calories you burn. The more you exercise and increase lean body mass, the easier it is to lose fat.

At the lab we put eighty people who were at least 20 percent overweight, according to the Metropolitan Life Insurance tables, on either a diet or a diet plus exercise. Both groups lost approximately eighteen pounds in four months. However, among the people who dieted without exercising, 25 percent of the pounds lost was lean tissue. Weight lost by people who walked and dieted was more than 85 percent fat. In fact, on a weight-loss program of diet alone, the pounds lost can be as high as 35 percent lean body mass. This helps set up for a yo-yo effect; with decreased lean body mass to burn up calories, a person inevitably puts on weight. And when weight is lost through dieting alone, there is even less lean body mass to burn off intake, so the weight comes back. In other words, not only does adding exercise to a diet help you lose weight, it also helps you maintain your weight loss.

Guidelines for Exercising When You're Overweight

The first step is to consult with your physician to determine how safe exercise is for you. Exercise is not for everyone. Your doctor should evaluate you to determine your body composition, flexibility, strength, and aerobic fitness.

How often and how intensely you need to exercise depends on your goals. For cardiovascular fitness you need to exercise more intensely; for weight loss you need to exercise for a longer time. To improve your cardiorespiratory fitness, you need to raise your heart rate to within 70 to 85 percent of your maximum heart rate for at least twenty to thirty minutes three to five times per week. On the other hand, you will burn more calories and lose more weight if you exercise longer and more frequently. To enable you to continue your exercise for a longer time, you should exercise at a lower intensity. For losing weight you need to raise your heart rate to 60 percent of your maximum rate five to seven days a week for forty to sixty minutes or more per day.

The Myths of Weight Loss

A common misconception about weight loss is that you can reduce specific parts of your body through exercise. "Spot reduction," as this is called, has definitely been proven not to occur. While exercising a particular body part will firm the muscles underneath the fat, it will not burn the fat off that spot any faster than it will off the rest of your body. Different bodies naturally store fat in different places, and you need to be realistic about the amount of sculpting you can do.

Sweating in saunas or rubber suits is not only futile, it can be dangerous. Though you will weigh less after a session in a sauna or rubber suit, what you have lost is water, not fat. You will regain the pounds as you replenish the water you have lost—usually within twenty-four hours, even if you don't drink extra liquids. To avoid dehydration—which can be dangerous—you should replenish the water you lose during exercise as soon as possible.

One of the oldest and most persistent myths about exercise is that it makes you hungry. Researchers report that people who exercise moderately eat less, not more, than people who are sedentary.

Many people, including volunteer research subjects we work with in our lab, have the misconception that walking is an undemanding exercise suitable only for people in their seventies and eighties. It usually takes only one fitness walk to show them how wrong that assumption is. In one study, volunteers between thirty and fifty years old found walking to be vigorous enough to raise their heart rate into the target training zone and to serve as an aerobic conditioner. We have shown the same results repeatedly in more than a thousand volunteer research subjects studied in our laboratory over the past five years. Fitness walking for a mile will elevate the heart rate into a target training zone for over 80 percent of individuals, regardless of age or level of conditioning.

How to Avoid Being a Dropout

Sticking to a weight-loss program takes the self-discipline of even the most resolute dieters. Finding a realistic program and enlivening it with some fun make it easier to stick with your plan. Observe the Four F's to help avoid being a dropout:

1. *Feasibility:* Find a diet and exercise program that is convenient, that you can fit into your lifestyle and your schedule.
2. *Flexibility:* Be sure to warm up and stretch in order to maintain flexibility and avoid injuries that could prevent you from exercising consistently.
3. *Faithfulness:* For maximum success you need to be faithful to your diet and walking program.
4. *Fun:* To help you follow your program on a daily basis, find a way to make your exercise fun.

9

WALKING AND TOTAL FITNESS

Aerobic exercise such as walking should serve as the cornerstone in your plan to reduce risk factors for heart disease. However, for total fitness, your plan should also include stretching exercises for flexibility and strength training for musculoskeletal strength and endurance.

Stretching

Stretching exercises develop and maintain an adequate range of motion in the body's joints, relieve stiffness, and prevent injuries. To enhance flexibility, stretch before and after exercise—at the beginning of the warm-up and at the end of the cool-down. These considerations will help you derive the most benefit from stretching:

• Select stretches that are specific for the exercise you are about to undertake. Analyze the muscle groups used in the sport or activity you plan to engage in and stretch those muscle groups. For example, walking and running use the large muscle groups at the front and back of the leg (quadriceps and hamstring muscles) as well as those of the lower back. Stretches should focus on these muscles. Other activities such as swimming and rowing involve arms and shoulders as well as back and leg muscles. It is important to think through your activity and prepare the particular muscles you will be using.

• Stretch slowly and gradually progress to greater ranges of motion. Move slowly into the stretch position, then sustain a static stretch for twenty to thirty seconds. You should never stretch to the point of actual pain. If at any point you experience pain, ease away from the stretch. Do not bounce up and down in the stretch; this practice, called "ballistic" stretching, can lead to injury.

• Breathe regularly. Focus on your breathing to help you relax and get the most out of your stretch. Breathe in and out regularly and avoid holding your breath.

The following stretches are appropriate for walkers:

Overhead Arm Reach

Stand with your feet shoulder-width apart with knees slightly bent. Extend both arms overhead. Reach up with first the left arm and then the right arm. Keep the movements slow as you stretch your arms overhead. Repeat six to eight times with each arm.

Side Bend/Stretch

From the Overhead Arm Reach position, place one hand on your hip. With the other arm overhead, bend slowly toward the hand on your hip. Hold the stretch for 10 to 15 seconds. Repeat on the other side. Repeat two to four times to each side.

Deltoid Stretch/Triceps Stretch

Stand with your feet shoulder-width apart with knees slightly bent.

1. Grasp elbow of right arm with left hand and pull right arm gently toward your left shoulder. Keep the right arm fairly straight during this stretch. Hold stretch for 10 to 15 seconds. Repeat with the other arm.

2. Extend the right arm overhead with the elbow near your right ear. Bend the arm at the elbow and hold the right elbow with the left hand. Gently pull the right elbow behind your head and hold the stretch for 15 to 30 seconds. Repeat with the other arm.

Inner Thigh Stretch

Stand with your feet about 3 feet apart. Have both feet facing directly forward. Bend the right knee and place the right hand on that knee. Shift your weight to the right side so that the right knee is directly over the right foot. Keep the left leg straight. Hold for 10 to 15 seconds. Repeat to the left side. Repeat two to four times to each side.

Bent-Knee Straddle Stretch

With both knees bent slightly in the Inner Thigh Stretch straddle position, bend forward from the hips and reach for the floor. Let your body relax as you hold this position. Hold for 20 to 30 seconds. Repeat Inner Thigh Stretch once on each leg. Now move your feet together until they are shoulder-width apart. Keeping your knees slightly bent, again bend forward from the hips and stretch for the floor. Hold for 20 to 30 seconds.

Calf Stretch

Begin the exercise with both feet together and pointing straight ahead. Take a big step forward with the right foot, bending that knee. Keep the left leg straight and keep the left heel/foot on the floor. Place both hands on the right knee or on a wall for balance. Move your hips forward toward your bent right knee until you feel a stretch in the calf of your left leg. Keep your toes pointed straight ahead. Hold for 15 to 30 seconds. Relax and repeat on the other leg. Repeat three to four times on each leg.

Additional Leg Stretches

From the above Calf Stretch position, bend the back knee a couple of inches and shift your weight slightly toward the back leg (it may help to slide the front foot back a few inches also). Hold for 15 to 30 seconds. From this position, straighten the front leg while bending the back knee more. Lean forward from the waist with your hands on your thighs for support. Point the toes of your front foot toward the ceiling. Hold for 15 to 30 seconds. Repeat the entire sequence with the other leg.

Standing Thigh Stretch

Hold on to a wall or pole for support. Stand on your left leg. Hold the top of your right foot with the left hand and gently pull the foot/heel toward your buttocks. The knee of the right leg should be pointing toward the floor. Hold the stretch for 15 to 30 seconds. Repeat with the other leg. Repeat two to four times on each side.

Standing Hamstring Stretch with Leg Up

Place one foot on a wall, chair, ledge, etc. Keep the supporting leg straight and have that foot also pointed straight ahead. Bend the knee of the "up" leg as you shift your hips forward. Move forward until you feel the stretch in your hamstrings and hips. Hold for 15 to 30 seconds with the knee bent. Slowly straighten the "up" leg and bend forward from the waist toward that leg until you feel the stretch in your hamstrings. Hold for 15 to 30 seconds. Repeat the sequence again with the same leg. Then switch legs and repeat twice on the other leg.

Foot/Ankle Circles

Stand with your weight mainly on one leg. Move the other foot in clockwise and counterclockwise circles to warm up the ankle. Do four to six circles in each direction. Then repeat with the other foot.

Musculoskeletal Strength Training

A well-rounded total fitness plan should also include musculoskeletal strength training. Increasing strength and muscular endurance improves your appearance by toning muscles, makes your aerobic training easier and more pleasant, improves your performance in recreational and leisure sports, and helps prevent injuries.

There are three basic types of regimes for building muscular strength and power: isometric, isotonic, and isokinetic. *Isometric* exercise involves contracting the muscle in one position against an immovable resistance, for example, pushing against a wall as hard as you can. Isometric training, which does not really enhance athletic performance, is not recommended since it sometimes raises blood pressure to dangerously high levels.

In *isotonic* exercise, the muscles contract through their full range of motion to overcome a fixed resistance, as in lifting weights, the classic isotonic exercise. Lifting weights builds strong and powerful muscles. It has one major limitation: Since muscles lift different amounts of weight at different angles, you are limited to lifting the amount of weight you can hoist through the weakest part of the range of motion of the particular muscle you are exercising.

Isokinetic exercise is performed on machines designed to overcome this problem. Weight systems like Lifecircuit,

Nautilus, Eagle, and Hydra-Fitness, which are found in many gyms and health clubs, have variable resistance against a fixed rate of contraction. This loads the muscle to its maximum capacity throughout its range of motion.

If you are beginning a strength training program, we strongly recommend that you get instruction from a qualified fitness specialist at an exercise facility. The specialist can help you choose a strength training system to suit your needs, teach you proper technique, and show you how to get started and how to progress. Proper instruction speeds progress and optimizes the benefits of strength training while also reducing the risk of injury.

Guidelines for Strength Training

You should do your strength training no more than three days per week (and not two days in a row) for fifteen to sixty minutes each time, either as part of an aerobic exercise session or on separate days. For maximum benefit allow the muscles you exercise a full day to recover before exercising them again. Base your specific strength training program on your needs and goals and the time and equipment available. For example, a walker who begins windsurfing—which demands strong arms and torso—should concentrate on his upper body in strength training. If you have high blood pressure or coronary heart disease or questions about the safety of muscle training for you, consult your physician.

Warm-up: Stretch for five or ten minutes before each strength training session. Be sure to stretch each muscle group you plan to exercise during the workout.

Frequency: Exercise each muscle group two or three times per week. Allow forty-eight hours between strength training workouts to give muscles time to recover. For example, a typical musculoskeletal strength building program would involve sessions on Monday, Wednesday, and Friday of a given week.

Intensity: The intensity of a strength training exercise depends on the amount of weight you lift and the number of times you lift it without resting. Each lift is called a *repetition* or *rep.* Consult an exercise specialist for advice about choosing a proper starting weight. The number of repetitions is based on your goals: lower weights and higher reps for strength and endurance; lower reps and higher weights for muscular bulk. For strength and endurance, select a weight you can lift eight to twelve times without resting.

Duration: Each group of eight to twelve reps is a *set.* The duration of your exercise is the number of sets you perform, which depends on the type of equipment you are using and the goals you have set for yourself. Tell your exercise specialist about your goals. Do you want to build bigger muscles? Do you want to tighten your midriff? Do you need to strengthen your ankles? Your specialist can recommend the best equipment for you to use and the number of sets to do to speed you toward your goal.

Progressive overload: To increase the size and strength of a muscle, you must overload it so that it works harder against greater resistance than it does with normal use. As you get stronger, the initial weights you used no longer overload the muscle. To continue to overload the muscle, you must increase the number of reps or the weight load.

Specificity: Only the muscle groups that are overloaded increase in strength and endurance. Although the specific groups you choose to exercise will be based on your goals and needs, in general we recommend a balanced program that exercises both the upper and lower body.

Breathing: Inhale with exertion and exhale when returning the weight to the starting position. Breathe regularly following this basic rhythm throughout each repetition.

To avoid injury, remember:

1. Never lift free weights alone. When you are working at maximum strength, your partner should be prepared to

FIGURE 13

Muscular Strength and Endurance Starter and Average Programs

Exercise	Muscles Used	Amount of Weight	Repetitions per Set	Starter (No. of Sets)	Average (No. of Sets)
Bench press	Chest	70% 1 RM*	10	1	2
Bent over rows	Back	70% 1 RM	10	1	2
Quadriceps extension	Quadriceps	70% 1 RM	10	1	2
Upright row	Shoulders	70% 1 RM	10	1	2
Hamstring curls	Hamstrings	70% 1 RM	10	1	2
Sit-ups	Abdominals	†	†	†	†
Biceps curl	Biceps	70% 1 RM	10	1	2
Toe raises with weights on shoulders	Calves	70% 1 RM	10	1	2
Triceps extension	Triceps	70% 1 RM*	10	1	2
Wrist curls	Forearms	70% 1 RM	10	1	2

*1 RM is the maximum amount of weight you can lift for one repetition.
†Start with 70% of the maximum number you can perform in 1 minute.
Reprinted from *Fit for Success: Proven Strategies for Exercise Health*, by James M. Rippe, M.D. Prentice Hall Press, New York, 1989.

Muscular Strength and Endurance Expert Program

Exercise	Muscles Used	Amount of Weight	Repetitions per Set	No. of Sets
Bench press	Chest	70% 1 RM*	10	3
Bent over rows	Back	70% 1 RM	10	3
Quadriceps extension	Quadriceps	70% 1 RM	10	3
Upright row	Shoulders	70% 1 RM	10	3
Hamstring curls	Hamstrings	70% 1 RM	10	3
Sit-ups	Abdominals	†	†	†
Biceps curl	Biceps	70% 1 RM	10	3
Toe raises with weights on shoulders	Calves	70% 1 RM	10	3
Triceps extension	Triceps	70% 1 RM	10	3
Wrist curls	Forearms	70% 1 RM	10	3

*1 RM is the maximum amount of weight you can lift for one repetition.
†Start with 70% of the maximum number you can perform in 1 minute.

Reprinted from *Fit for Success: Proven Strategies for Exercise Health*, by James M. Rippe, M.D. Prentice Hall Press, New York, 1989.

"spot" you by giving you help if you are caught under too much weight.

2. Use proper mechanics. Think about which muscle group you are working during each exercise. Use weights that allow you to control the movement so that you do not involve extraneous body parts in lifting the weight. If you are working parts of your body that should not be involved, choose a lower weight.

3. Use consistent rhythm during the set and do not pause between reps.

4. *Progress slowly!*

A simplified program of ten exercises that utilize all of the body's major muscle groups is shown below. The exact equipment you use will vary according to the facilities available to you.

WALKING FOR CHILDREN

In 1954 a famous research project by Kraus and Hirschland reported that American school children were less fit than their European counterparts. This sparked such serious concern across the nation that President Eisenhower founded the President's Council on Physical Fitness. Through the 1950s and 1960s, physical education programs in the schools expanded to remedy this serious problem. Many of the children who profited by those programs are today's middle-aged adults who have continued walking or jogging for their health.

Although the President's Council continues to test school children and to present the Presidential Fitness Award to those scoring high on this test, major new studies show that our children's physical fitness is declining, not improving. According to the 1985 National Children and Youth Fitness Study, published by the U.S. Department of Health and Human Services, at least a third of the young people in this country are not physically active enough for aerobic benefit. Overall, young children weigh more and have more body fat than they did twenty years ago.

At the same time, tight school budgets and curriculum requirements have led to cuts in physical education programs. In 1964, 90 percent of tenth-graders had regular physical education; by 1988 the figure had dropped to 69 percent. Only five state school systems require physical education in all grades, and only Illinois requires daily physical education. At a time when the American College of Sports Medicine has called for school programs of twenty to thirty minutes of vigorous exercise a day for students in all grades, only 36 percent of all children in this country have daily physical education.

America needs to restore physical education in the schools, and we also need to review the current physical education programs. For many years schools promoted strength, agility, and speed without distinguishing the fitness needed for athletic performance from that required for health. The stringent, performance-oriented tests for the Presidential Fitness Award include pull-ups for boys, modified pull-ups for girls, sit-ups, a standing long jump, a 30-yard shuttle run, a 50-yard dash, a 600-yard run, and a softball throw. Emphasis is on skills needed to play basketball or football, with no reference to cardiorespiratory endurance, balanced body composition, flexibility, and overall muscular strength and endurance, which contribute to good health and functioning in daily life.

This confusion between sports fitness and health has led many adults to encourage the athletically talented young people—about 15 percent of the youth population—to be physically active while ignoring the basic needs of all children to exercise for their health. In fact, many sports performance factors, most of which depend on genetic predisposition, are insignificant in the day-to-day lives of Americans. Even the students who participated in games like football or basketball at school seldom participate in them as adults. One value of teaching children fundamental motor

skills—the ABCs of movement—is that these skills may encourage them to participate in games, dances, and sports
that will improve their aerobic fitness as adults.

How serious is the problem? Many children cannot perform elementary exercises. More than 50 percent of girls
aged six to seventeen and 30 percent of boys aged six to
twelve cannot run a mile in less than ten minutes. What
about musculoskeletal strength? Seventy percent of girls and
40 percent of boys six to twelve years of age cannot do even
one pull-up. Obesity in children six to eleven has increased
by 54 percent in the last twenty years alone.

All children, like all adults, need physical activity as
part of an overall program to prevent heart disease. For
many years scientists thought the risk factors for heart disease—elevated cholesterol, high blood pressure, and
obesity—were conditions occurring in middle age. We now
realize these problems begin in childhood. A child who has
high blood pressure is very likely to have high blood pressure fifteen years later when he is an adult. The same is true
of high cholesterol; one alarming study at the University of
Michigan showed 25 percent of children had elevated blood
cholesterol. Between 15 and 25 percent of American school
children are obese—and 80 percent of obese children become obese adults. The most alarming statistic of all is that
by the age of twelve between 40 and 50 percent of all children have developed at least one major risk factor for heart
disease.

Fortunately, young people who exercise lower the risk of
cardiovascular disease—just as adults do. Perhaps even
more important, young people who exercise develop the
habit of being physically active, which helps alleviate the
risks of heart disease throughout their lives.

While adults who recognize they are at risk of heart
disease often start a walking program or join a health club to
get the exercise they need, young people must rely on the
wisdom and concern of their parents and community. Our
first goal should be to nurture the natural pleasure little

children take in physical activity to encourage it to flower in adulthood.

If schools have restricted time and money for physical education, then the responsibility for getting young people to be active falls on family and community. However, several circumstances in our daily lives hinder young people from participating in vigorous physical activity. Children who remain at home alone after school often stay indoors with the door locked for safety. Crowded urban neighborhoods offer other children limited space for physical activity. Above all, television lures children into a sedentary lifestyle. A number of researchers have found that young people's excessive television viewing fosters inactivity and obesity, the leading cause of hypertension. In fact, one recent study showed that in the overall population of adolescents, each hourly increment in watching television was associated with a 2-percent increase in the prevalence of obesity.

The National Child Youth Fitness Study Part II released by the U.S. Department of Health and Human Services in 1987 revealed how the habits of parents are reflected in their children: Children of sedentary parents tend to be sedentary, children of active parents usually are active. The number of hours young people watched television reflected how many hours their parents watched television. Less than 50 percent of parents exercise with their children for twenty minutes a week, while children watch television on average more than two hours per weekday and three hours and twenty-six minutes per day on the weekend. Since sedentary children seldom participate in organized sports in their community, they must rely on their parents to encourage them to turn off the television and spend more time exercising. And since a sedentary lifestyle can be fairly habitual by the time a child is eleven years old, the importance of early intervention cannot be exaggerated.

The most effective way for parents to persuade their children to be physically active is to become physically active themselves and arrange for their children to join them.

Walking is an excellent exercise for parents and children to do together. We have already noted that walking is a convenient and almost risk-free exercise for improving cardiovascular fitness and losing weight—the primary goals of sedentary people. Walking is not competitive, and it's good for all children regardless of age, size, or level of fitness. Our lab has recently received a major research grant from the Ronald McDonald Children's Charities to develop a new youth walking test much like the one we developed for adults. (Later in this chapter we will describe the youth walking test we developed.)

How can we encourage children to walk? The first thing we need to do is to get young people interested in physical activity. In the long run young people are most likely to follow the example of their parents. Family walks can incorporate a picnic, a special destination, or even an overnight stay in the woods—whatever makes them fun. Walking together requires some adjustments in pace for younger and slower walkers, but the rewards will be worth the adjustment. Walks encourage children to socialize with their parents in new ways, and they open opportunities for teaching kids about whatever they see along the way.

Although it takes some imagination to keep children motivated to walk, the rewards are great. Not only will your children get healthier and leaner, walking together may open new avenues of communication.

As all parents know, with small children little problems can disrupt pleasant occasions. Here are some practical suggestions about how to avoid some of those pitfalls and keep your family walk on target:

• To avoid overdoing it with beginning walkers, plan the walk, including the destination and the length of time the walk will take.

• Tell the children ahead of time so they can be thinking about the walk. Anticipation is part of the fun and puts children in the frame of mind to walk.

• Be prepared with water or juice, Band-Aids, tissues, and an extra sweater. A tiny scratch unattended, a little thirst unquenched, a chilly breeze can destroy an otherwise promising walk.

• Think ahead of games, songs, and other ways to keep interest high once the walk has begun.

• Take along plastic bags to collect interesting bugs or rocks or whatever catches the children's attention.

• Keep in mind that children love to say "I'm tired," and it takes a little sympathy and distraction to keep them going.

• Children cannot walk very far or very fast. Remember those painful side stitches you had when you were a child? Set a pace and a course that are realistic.

Children may or may not be interested in going for a walk for fitness, but they always respond to an interesting destination, a challenging hunt, creative games that involve walking, and singing songs as they walk along. They may love walking to the fire department, around a museum or a hospital, to a beaver pond, on a beach, up a hill, or to visit a friend. Keeping a record of where you've been and how far you have walked is fun and encourages children to look forward to another walk. Try to keep the games noncompetitive. (Who can find a penny? How many paces is it between utility poles?) The object is to get and keep children walking. One hundred percent participation is the ideal.

A Fitness-Walking Test for Children

The walking-test norms were developed by the Division of Cardiovascular Medicine at the University of Massachusetts Medical Center in Worcester and the Exercise Science Department at U Mass/Amherst. More than 380 six- to thirteen-year-old children were tested to develop the norms.

STEP ONE: ADMINISTERING THE TEST

1. The walking test is a half-mile distance for the six- to nine-year-old children and a one-mile walk for the ten- to thirteen-year-old children.

2. Locate a quarter-mile track or some other known flat distance so that you'll be able to determine exactly a half-mile or a mile.

3. Be sure to have the children stretch for five to ten minutes before doing the walking test, focusing on stretches for the legs and lower back.

4. Participants will walk either a half-mile (children six to nine years) or a mile (children ten to thirteen years) as rapidly as possible while maintaining a constant pace. In other words, speed should be the maximum speed that can be maintained throughout the entire walk (be sure to caution kids not to run). It might be necessary to practice so that the children understand the concept of pacing, which is very important for accurate test results.

5. Record time at the end of the walk in minutes and seconds. The half-mile should generally take between five and ten minutes and the mile should take between ten and twenty minutes.

6. Following completion of the tests, participants should cool down by walking, at a slow pace, for two to three minutes followed by five minutes of stretching.

STEP TWO: INTERPRETATION OF TEST RESULTS

1. Turn to the Walk-Time Categories (below) and identify the appropriate age and gender category. Note that there are no gender-specific norms for the six- to nine-year-old children. The reason for this is that in our study there were no significant differences in walk time between the boys and girls.

2. Match the individual's walk time with the color categories for the appropriate age group.

3. Turn to the appropriate color-coded walking program.

4. The child is now ready to begin his or her walking program.

5. Complete the walk test again after eighteen sessions of the walking program or after eighteen sessions of any other type of regular physical activity program in order to measure improvement in walk time.

Children who are closer in age to the next age category should be considered to fall in the younger age group. For example, a child who is six years eleven months old will fall in the six-year-old age category.

HALF-MILE WALK-TIME CATEGORIES

AGE	RED	GREEN	PURPLE
6–7 YEARS	≤7:15	7:16–8:40	≥8:41
8–9 YEARS	≤6:40	6:41–8:00	≥8:01

ONE-MILE WALK-TIME CATEGORIES

AGE	BLUE	ORANGE	YELLOW
10–11 YEARS			
BOYS	≤12:45	12:46–16:00	≥16:01
GIRLS	≤13:20	13:21–16:10	≥16:11
12–13 YEARS			
BOYS	≤12:20	12:21–15:05	≥15:06
GIRLS	≤12:55	12:56–15:10	≥15:11

Walking Programs for Children

If the child walks for the time indicated, for the given distance, pace will be as shown. For example, a child who walks for nine minutes and travels 0.50 mile is walking at a pace of 3.3 miles per hour. It may be difficult to teach kids about pace, and it may also be difficult to monitor pace. Therefore, using time and distance as guidelines for walking are more appropriate. Be flexible and adapt these programs accordingly.

PROGRAM FOR CHILDREN 6–9 YEARS

RED PROGRAM

PHASE	1	2	3	4	5	6
WARM-UP (min)	5	5	5	5	5	5
TIME (min)	9	12	15	18	21	24
DISTANCE (mi)	0.5	0.7	0.9	1.1	1.3	1.5
PACE (mph)	3.3	3.5	3.6	3.7	3.7	3.75
COOL-DOWN (min)	5	5	5	5	5	5

GREEN PROGRAM

PHASE	1	2	3	4	5	6
WARM-UP (min)	5	5	5	5	5	5
TIME (min)	9	12	15	18	21	24
DISTANCE (mi)	0.4	0.6	0.8	1	1.2	1.4
PACE (mph)	2.7	3	3.2	3.3	3.4	3.5
COOL-DOWN (min)	5	5	5	5	5	5

PURPLE PROGRAM

PHASE	1	2	3	4	5	6
WARM-UP (min)	5	5	5	5	5	5
TIME (min)	9	12	15	18	21	24
DISTANCE (mi)	0.3	0.5	0.7	0.9	1.1	1.3
PACE (mph)	2	2.5	2.8	3	3.1	3.25
COOL-DOWN (min)	5	5	5	5	5	5

PROGRAM FOR CHILDREN 10–13 YEARS

BLUE PROGRAM

PHASE	1	2	3	4	5	6
WARM-UP (min)	5	5	5	5	5	5
TIME (min)	9	12	15	18	21	24
DISTANCE (mi)	0.6	0.8	1	1.2	1.4	1.6
PACE (mph)	4	4	4	4	4	4
COOL-DOWN (min)	5	5	5	5	5	5

ORANGE PROGRAM

PHASE	1	2	3	4	5	6
WARM-UP (min)	5	5	5	5	5	5
TIME (min)	9	12	15	18	21	24
DISTANCE (mi)	0.5	0.7	0.9	1.1	1.3	1.5
PACE (mph)	3.3	3.5	3.6	3.7	3.7	3.75
COOL-DOWN (min)	5	5	5	5	5	5

YELLOW PROGRAM

PHASE	1	2	3	4	5	6
WARM-UP (min)	5	5	5	5	5	5
TIME (min)	9	12	15	18	21	24
DISTANCE (mi)	0.4	0.6	0.8	1	1.2	1.4
PACE (mph)	2.7	3	3.2	3.3	3.4	3.5
COOL-DOWN (min)	5	5	5	5	5	5

For ten- to thirteen-year-olds, you can establish the speed of walking sessions so that the participant is walking at a speed corresponding to a percentage of maximum heart rate, the so-called target heart rate (discussed in Chapter 2). The target heart rate has been shown to represent the intensity of exercise associated with cardiovascular fitness in adults. In other words, if an individual uses the target heart-rate as a "speedometer" during regular walk training, a cardiovascular training effect may occur. To monitor heart rate, have participants walk at a pace you show them for five minutes, then stop and take heart rate for fifteen seconds.

The fifteen-second values should fall into a certain percentage of age-predicted maximum heart rate; use the range of 31 to 44 beats per fifteen seconds. This corresponds to between 60 and 85 percent of age-predicted maximum heart rate.

TARGET HEART RATES FOR 10- TO 13-YEAR OLDS

PERCENTAGE OF AGE-PREDICTED MAXIMUM HEART RATE	HEART-RATE RANGE (BEATS PER MIN)	HEART-RATE RANGE (BEATS PER 15 SEC)
60–65%	123–137	31–34
66–70%	138–147	35–37
71–75%	148–158	38–40
76–80%	159–168	41–42
81–85%	169–178	43–44

For example, if you select 60 to 65 percent as the target intensity, then the child's fifteen-second heart rate should be between 31 and 34 immediately following a five-minute walk at a steady pace. If the child's heart rate is less than the prescribed heart-rate intensity, have the child increase speed and reevaluate heart rate after walking for five minutes at the faster speed. If the child's heart rate is greater than the prescribed heart-rate intensity, have the child slow down and reevaluate heart rate after walking for five minutes at the slower speed.

Follow these guidelines for establishing target heart rate:

1. If the child is in the Yellow program, use 60 to 70 percent for Phases 1 and 2, 71 to 75 percent for Phases 3 and 4, and 76 to 85 percent for Phases 5 and 6, and then maintain at 76 to 85 percent beyond Phase 6.

2. If the child is in the Orange program, use 66 to 70 percent for Phases 1 and 2, 71 to 80 percent for Phases 3 and

4, and 81 to 85 percent for Phases 5 and 6, and then maintain at 81 to 85 percent beyond Phase 6.

3. If the child is in the Blue program, use 71 to 75 percent for Phases 1 and 2, 76 to 85 percent for Phases 3 and 4, and 81 to 85 percent for Phases 5 and 6, and then maintain at 81 to 85 percent beyond Phase 6.

WALKING AND WELL-BEING

Keeping Your Cardiac Risk Factors Low

The death of runner Jim Fixx called attention to what we have known all along, that exercise is not the total solution to the problem of heart disease. Scientific studies show that walking lowers your level of anxiety, expedites weight loss, decreases the risk of cardiovascular diseases, and assists in recovery from them. But inactivity is only one of several risk factors that predispose people to heart disease, and walking is no "magic bullet" that eliminates all these risks.

Three major risk factors predispose a person to heart disease and five factors have been classified as minor. The *major risk factors* are cigarette smoking, elevated blood cholesterol, and high blood pressure. The *minor risk factors* are an inactive lifestyle, a family history of coronary heart disease, diabetes, stress, and obesity.

Unfortunately, the major risk factors don't just add up, they multiply. That is, with one major risk factor, you have twice the probability of developing heart disease as a person with no risk factors. With two major risk factors, your chances quadruple; with all three major risk factors, the chances increase eight times. The good news is that all of the major risk factors and three of the minor ones are under your control. You can change them. And just as they multiply when you add one to another, so when you control one, you minimize the others. Furthermore, research indicates that when you get one habit under control, a ripple effect makes it easier to deal with the others. Let's look at each risk factor, starting with the major ones, and the impact that walking can have on each one.

MAJOR RISK FACTORS

Smoking: During the mid-1980s Surgeon General Everett Koop issued increasingly alarming bulletins about the hazards of smoking cigarettes. Smoking is the single major cause of preventable deaths and disease in America. Cigarette smokers are thirty times more likely to develop lung cancer than nonsmokers. Smoking more than a pack of cigarettes a day triples the chances of a heart attack.

Why are cigarettes bad for your heart? Two of the products of cigarettes and cigarette smoke—nicotine and carbon monoxide—are related to heart disease. Nicotine is a mild stimulant that raises the heart rate, increases blood pressure, and makes the heart vulnerable to rhythm disturbances. It plays a direct role in increasing free fatty acids in the blood and in increasing the stickiness of platelets, the blood's main clotting elements. Carbon monoxide starves the heart and body tissues of oxygen.

Fortunately, the risk of heart disease drops by 50 percent within one year after a smoker quits, and after ten years the risk approaches that of a nonsmoker. According to the College Alumni Study, active and fit people are less likely to smoke than those who are sedentary and less fit. In every category—from people who never smoked and former smokers to light, moderate, heavy, and very heavy smokers—those who exercise have a lower risk of developing coronary heart disease than do sedentary people in the same smoking category. While walking cannot stop people from smoking, the discipline that impels walking can be harnessed to stop this destructive habit. The American Heart, Lung, and Cancer associations all provide information and run programs to help smokers quit.

Blood cholesterol: Hardly a person in the United States can have missed the recent public discussions of cholesterol and the role it plays in cardiovascular disease. Scientists now know there is beneficial as well as detrimental cholesterol and that people need to keep "bad" cholesterol in check. Cholesterol is wrapped in different kinds of lipoproteins. When hidden in the smallest lipoproteins, called high-density lipoproteins (HDL), "good" cholesterol is safely carried to the liver to be excreted or made into bile acid. "Bad" cholesterol, wrapped in low-density lipoproteins (LDL), is delivered to the cells but on the way it can also stick to artery walls, where it accumulates, narrowing the passage for blood. A recent study found that postal workers who walk several miles per day had increased levels of good HDL, which helps lower the levels of "bad" cholesterol.

Since there are no special symptoms for high cholesterol, you must have it checked by a physician. Knowing your cholesterol level should become as routine as being aware of your blood pressure.

Hypertension: Scientists have had difficulty identifying the exact, underlying cause of hypertension, though the improper handling of salt by the kidneys seems to be a large part of the problem. Reducing salt intake is the first line of defense in lowering your blood pressure. Physical activity reduces both obesity and stress, two other conditions often associated with hypertension.

MINOR RISK FACTORS

Inactive lifestyle: According to a recent report from the Centers for Disease Control (CDC), inactivity, which contributes to several of the other risk factors for heart disease, increases the risk of heart disease as much as smoking a pack of cigarettes a day. In fact, the CDC study showed that inactive people *double* their risk of heart disease compared to active individuals.

Diabetes: Not only can walking reduce the amount of insulin a diabetic needs, it lowers the danger of heart disease, which is the chief cause of death among diabetics.

Stress: Many people who find they are under heavy pressure at home or on the job feel that they can't take time to exercise. In fact, the busier a person is, the more he or she needs to make time to exercise. Exercise increases stamina and helps people cope with stress.

Obesity: While many people are concerned about their weight, few people realize that obesity can cut years off their lives. People who are 40 percent overweight at age fifty—and many people are—die an average of ten years earlier than people with normal weight. We've already established earlier in the book the positive benefits of walking on weight loss.

Alcohol: Alcohol can become a serious problem, contributing to a variety of gastrointestinal problems ranging from liver diseases, particularly the often fatal cirrhosis of the liver, to bleeding ulcers and esophageal cancer. Alcohol causes many automobile accidents and contributes to many homicides and suicides. Even so, the Surgeon General recommended drinking moderately rather than giving up alcohol entirely. Alcohol causes mild and consistent elevations in the good lipoproteins, thus providing some protection against heart disease. Moderation is essential, however. That means no more than one five-ounce glass of wine or one and a half ounces of liquor such as you would have in a highball or one or two beers on a daily basis. If you are trying to lose weight, one good reason not to drink at all is that alcohol is loaded with calories and has virtually no nutritional value.

The Surgeon General's Report

Cardiovascular disease is not the only serious health problem we could alleviate by exercise and better nutrition. According to the Surgeon General's Report on Nutrition and Health issued in 1988, eight of the ten leading causes of death in this country—heart disease, cancer, strokes, injuries, diabetes, suicide, liver disease, and atherosclerosis—are related to diet and alcohol. The report recommends that we change five aspects of our diet and lifestyle to help control these diseases. We need to: eat less fat and cholesterol; exercise and control our weight; eat more carbohydrates and fiber; eat less salt; and consume less alcohol.

Like the Surgeon General's report of 1965, which warned people about smoking cigarettes, this report may take time to have an effect. But that famous earlier report helped reduce dramatically the number of people who smoke and to change the way society views smoking. As we begin to put into practice the 1988 report's recommendations on nutrition and exercise, it may have a similar impact on our society—but this time on the way we eat, drink, and exercise. Already many people under treatment for high blood pressure have reduced their use of salt, and several food companies are providing foods with reduced sodium. And alcohol consumption is down. The report has heightened our awareness of the danger of high cholesterol and the importance of eating more carbohydrates and fiber.

12

FITTING IT IN: HOW TO MAKE WALKING A PART OF YOUR DAILY LIFE

Once you begin your walking program, motivation becomes the key to success. Within six months of beginning most exercise programs, 50 percent of the participants drop out. Studies indicate that walking programs have a much higher rate of adherence, but the early days of your walking program are critical.

You'll need extra discipline to overcome several natural obstacles during the first week. If you have not exercised for some time, you will be very tired after the first few walks and your muscles will get sore and stiff. Adjusting your daily habits and routine to include your walking schedule is often awkward at first. Worst of all, at the beginning you won't yet enjoy the increased self-esteem and the improved cardiovascular fitness that is the reward for walking.

One strategy for keeping your spirits high is a weekly review of your motives for walking and its benefits. Most walkers cite motives like improving cardiovascular fitness, losing weight, staying fit for athletic competitions; you may have others, like seeing a friend or enjoying nature or the sights of the city. Other benefits include reduced stress, better concentration, fewer negative emotions, greater stamina, better emotional balance, more energy, and weight loss. The more precise you can be, the better. Take a piece of paper and write down your answers to such questions as: Do you feel less irritable? Can you stay with your work longer with less fatigue? Did you lose a pound last week? Can you walk up two flights of stairs without panting? Is it easier to climb in and out of the car? Do you suffer fewer minor aches and pains?

On another sheet of paper list the factors that undermine your motivation. The weather? Reluctance to leave your work? Boredom? Knowing these factors alerts you to what's going on in your mind and helps you to weigh these obstacles against the benefits of walking.

Always remember that you have a choice about what you do with your time and energy. By beginning a walking program you have already accepted this idea, but now you should examine it more directly. Even if you feel pressed by responsibilities toward work, family, and community, *you* ultimately decide whether or not to make room in your life for new choices, new possibilities, and new growth. These decisions can be disconcerting because you are taking control instead of allowing circumstances and other people to run your life.

Respect yourself enough to follow through with your commitment to your own program. You have chosen to begin walking because of its physical and mental benefits. In following through with the program, you are not only respecting your own needs, but you are honoring a promise you have made to yourself. When you don't follow through, you are concentrating on obstacles rather than benefits.

To compensate for some of walking's minor discomforts, add some agreeable things to your walk. Find a convenient time to walk so that it fits into your schedule, vary your route, enlist the support of your spouse or a friend, don't overdo it, warm up and cool down to avoid injury, get good walking shoes, walk inside during bad weather, reward yourself for your faithfulness to the program.

Though you may need these strategies to reinforce your resolve, remind yourself that walking will soon become habitual, and ultimately you may become one of millions of people positively addicted to fitness walking.

Walking at Home

Since we generally organize our houses to save as many steps as possible, one simple way to incorporate more walking is to disorganize ourselves a little bit. Simply put: Don't be so efficient. For example, if you have to climb stairs to move things, do it item by item, not all at once. Get rid of a couple of extension phones so you'll have to walk farther to answer a call. Instead of having your children or someone else run errands for you, go get your own sweater, mow your own lawn, climb the step ladder to replace a light bulb. Put all this together and you have included a lot more walking in your daily activities.

Consider leaving the car behind and going on foot where ordinarily you would drive. Since almost everybody has to run errands, begin by thinking about what you have to do and how much of it you can do on foot. Is it possible to walk to the bank? The post office? Could you get a cart with wheels to carry your groceries home so you could walk to the store? If walking from your house is not possible, perhaps you could drive to a place that makes walking possible, and walk from there; your walk begins at the car, includes all your errands, and ends back at the car.

If you chart your neighborhood with a pedometer instead of the odometer on your car, you'll have taken a long walk as well as laid out routes for future walks. Lay out short and long routes through as many different streets or paths as possible. Include on your chart a walk to a friend's house, then walk together instead of sitting over a cup of coffee. If you take a young child along on your walks, consider getting a stroller with soft, fat tires to absorb bumps so you won't have to slow down because of rough pavement or loose gravel. Once in a while get a group of friends together to walk. Take your dog for a walk. You will have a grateful and tireless companion.

Walking at Work

You may find it convenient to do more walking at your workplace. For a quick refresher, take a walk instead of eating a doughnut during your coffee break. Lunchtime is often long enough for a regular fitness walk that will make you feel better all afternoon. You can also incorporate walking into your daily habits by taking the stairs in your building instead of the elevator, and parking your car some way from your work and walking before and after work.

Some people find that discussion with colleagues during a walk opens lines of communication. One CEO we interviewed said he found out what his employees were thinking while he exercised with them. Since walking changes perspective and reduces tension, some people walk together while they are thrashing out problems at work. One dramatically successful example: Before Israel and Egypt signed the peace accords in 1979, Anwar Sadat and Menachem Begin left the negotiating table and resolved crucial sticking points during their famous "walk in the woods" at Camp David.

But it need not be all work. One appealing thing about walking at work is that you can probably recruit one or more of your colleagues to join you just for fun. While a regular companion bolsters your own commitment to your walking program, spur-of-the-moment walkers add variety, so don't feel let down if you have to look around for different people to walk with. If you discover that several colleagues are interested in walking, you could start a company walking club. A club provides some structure and builds morale and it may be the ideal way to involve more people in walking. A company fitness program improves morale, increases communication, and reduces absenteeism. You may find your employer an enthusiastic supporter of such a project.

To build up interest in walking, give your club a name like Put Your Heart Into It or Laughing All the Way. Remind people that walking is fun and social as well as healthful.

Set a time and place early in your plans. Count on a total of thirty minutes so that you can include warm-up and cooldown and twenty minutes of fitness walking. Lunchtime is ideal, but before or after work or between shifts is sometimes more convenient.

Remind people they should come prepared to walk in all but the most severe weather. Try to find an indoor route in your building if there is space or in a nearby mall for days when the weather prevents you from walking outside.

Chart a course. Use your car's odometer or a pedometer to lay out a one- to four-mile course through city streets, parks, meadows, woods, or indoor malls or walkways. Keep abreast of the urban trails that may be developed in the neighborhood of your workplace.

Take your first club walk as soon as possible after you announce the formation of the club. A workable schedule may be something like this: The first week announce the club's formation, the second week hold an introductory meeting, the third week go for a walk. At the introductory meeting explain the program and show people how to find their target heart rate. You may want to bring in an expert like a walking-shoe company representative or a doctor interested in sports medicine to lead the group.

If possible, celebrate the first walk by giving everybody a balloon or a hat or a T-shirt or some memento to mark the day.

Tap into local resources for advice and sponsorship. A hospital, health club, YMCA, the company medical department, a college or high school physical education department, or the local recreation department may provide information about how to prepare a walking program. A local sports store may be interested in your program and may offer some incentives.

For some people walking is the best part of their jobs. A letter carrier in one hilly town in Virginia chose the steepest route because he said he enjoyed the "walker's high," and he liked to be outside. A waitress, fit and middle-aged, thinks sitting at a desk all day would be deadly and loves the brisk walking required to get the customers' food to them while it's hot. A young courier in the city enjoys the exercise and the variety of people and places he sees as he walks through the city every day.

Staying with It

Exercising is like buying a new house. In the beginning you struggle to make a down payment and you face a thirty-year mortgage. The goal seems remote and the obstacles formidable. After the initial expenses, however, you move in, and those payments become automatic and secondary to the pleasure of living in your own house. In fact, the payments give you a sense of accomplishment because every one is another step toward owning your own home.

As you begin looking that exercise program in the face, remember that one day sooner or later—and probably sooner—you will be sorely tempted to put it aside for today or tomorrow or this week. The Public Health Service reports that only 25 percent of those who exercise regularly have done so for five years or more. Staying with it is the key to success. Growing old is not for the fainthearted, someone once said, and we would add that if you are fainthearted, you may never have the chance to grow old. You need some discipline to pursue your fitness-walking program, the cornerstone of a healthy life.

Here are six old and tattered excuses for allowing a walking program to lapse:

"I'm too busy; I don't have time."

We all know that we find time to do what we want to do and what we must do. Put your fitness-walking program on the "must do" list for twenty weeks, and it probably will slide onto the "want to do" list all by itself. Fitness walking relieves the stress of a busy schedule and gives you the stamina you need to do all the things you have to do.

"Walking is so inconvenient."

The problem is, you haven't satisfactorily integrated your walking schedule with the rest of your schedule. Everyone has to get from one place to another in the course of a week. Try walking instead of driving the car or taking the train or bus. Use the stairs instead of the elevator.

"Walking hurts my bad knee."

Begin with an okay from your doctor and some strength and flexibility exercises to help the injured joint. If you pursue it carefully, walking is one of the best exercises to rehabilitate a bad knee.

"My walking program cuts into my family time."

If possible, include your whole family in your fitness walking and make it a good time to be together. Getting your children involved in walking while they are young establishes a priceless lifelong habit. Even if your family doesn't come along at first, they may well be intrigued by the changes fitness walking makes in your appearance and attitude and want to join you later.

"Walking is boring."

Walking is one of the most versatile exercises you can adopt. Choose a different course, look for different things,

begin hiking in the woods, walk through a new neighborhood, the park, or the city streets. Join a group or form a
group. Or go by yourself for a change and let this be a time to
let your mind wander.

"Exercise has to hurt to provide results."
Walking explodes this myth. Major recent medical studies indicate that it is consistency, not intensity that makes a
walking program effective. You don't need to wake up sore
all over to achieve cardiac health, and once you develop the
habit, the exertion becomes easier.

Instead of indulging in excuses, use these tips to help
you stay with it:

• Adopt a specific plan and write it down. One of the
advantages of the Rockport Fitness Walking Test exercise
program outlined in Chapter 2 is that it provides a plan so
you can chart your progress. The walking test in Chapter 2
will get you started at the right level. Many exercise programs falter during periods of transition when you reach one
goal and are not sure how you want to proceed. This fitness-
walking program provides a plan that never leaves you un-
certain about what to do next.

• Set realistic goals. At the end of our weight-loss experiment, one of the volunteers said, "I am at peace with
food for the first time." The reason she was at peace was that
she had rejected the unrealistic goal of losing ten pounds by
next Tuesday and set a realistic target weight for herself. She
had adopted a new workable diet and a fitness-walking program to help her reach her target weight and maintain it.

• Get a pair of good walking shoes. Walking shoes not
only save you from blisters and strain, they are a sign of your
commitment to your fitness-walking program. When you put
them on, they put you in the right frame of mind to walk.

• Establish a definite time and place. What you are
trying to do is establish a new habit, and one of the best

props you can use is regularity. Having a regular time and place to walk also makes it easier to integrate fitness walking into your schedule.

• Enlist the support of family and friends. Since walking allows conversation, your fitness walk can be a great way to spend time with a friend or spouse. Even if no one walks with you, your family and friends can give you moral support by showing interest in your progress.

• Plan to vary your walk. If your program of fitness walking is disrupted before it is firmly established, your resolve may weaken. For example, you begin fitness walking in April and walk five days a week all through the spring and early summer. Then comes a July day when it's 90 degrees. One hot day stretches into two and then into a heat wave and your walking program goes up in steam. Plan ahead for those bad days. When you first begin walking, realize the time will come when you will need an indoor route and find a mall or atrium or even a stairwell where you can walk when the weather is bad.

• Avoid injury by warming up before and cooling down after your walk. Do stretching exercises after your warm-up and as part of your cool-down because warm ligaments and tendons are less vulnerable to sprains. Walking rarely produces injuries, but a sprained ankle is painful and can put you out of commission and disrupt your program.

• Keep a log of your progress. You have set specific goals for yourself and the next logical step is to keep a record of your progress toward those goals. Your log will motivate and challenge you by showing you how far you've come, and it will help you plan the next walk.

• Upgrade your fitness program as you progress. If you are following the walking program outlined in Chapter 2, then the phases are graduated to suit your increased levels of fitness. When you finish one of the color-coded exercise programs in the Rockport Fitness Walking Program, test yourself and immediately move into the next program. In some instances you will need to move into the middle range (weeks 8 to 10) of the next program to keep a smooth progression going.

• Reward yourself for a job well done. The major reward for improving your lifestyle is better health, better mental outlook, better endurance, and better looks. But when you work hard toward specific goals, like the end of one twenty-week program, you should earn an extra dividend—a book or compact disk you particularly want, a new piece of walking gear—whatever will show you that you appreciate the work you have done and what you have accomplished.

First, however, you must begin. Research has shown that if you stick with a walking program for six months, you are likely to stay with it a lifetime, but it has also shown that if you get through this initial six-month period, even if you lapse for a time, you are very likely to return to your program and try again. Like every journey, the journey to a healthy lifestyle begins with a single step.

THE WORLD OF
WALKING

Walking Clubs

Walking clubs existed long before the fitness walking boom of the 1980s. One of the oldest, the 115-year-old Appalachian Mountain Club, like most of the early clubs, was founded to create and maintain trails and shelters in the mountains for hikers who came from the city. The Sierra Club, founded in 1892, was concerned with preserving the wilderness as well as providing for the welfare of hikers. In Germany, walking clubs were founded in the last century when running events became too competitive for members whose goal was to exercise and enjoy walking without the pressure of racing. The purpose of these clubs was to lay out routes and organize events in which everybody could participate.

As people explore more ways to enjoy walking, many kinds of clubs have evolved which provide structure, companionship, and variety. These organizations vary from small, informal groups of friends walking together to international associations that sponsor special walking events.

There are more than 1,300 organizations in the United States and Canada for walkers of every kind—mall walkers, race walkers, volksmarchers, senior striders, day hikers, and serious backpackers. It's likely you can find a club nearby that offers the kind of walking you like to do. (See the list of walking clubs in the Appendix.)

If you don't find a nearby club, you may want to start one of your own, sharing your information and enthusiasm about walking with others. Walk leaders not only organize the program, they encourage and inspire other members to stick with their walking program. Work through your local health club, or YMCA, a community group, a local business, church, or school to find a group of people interested in forming a walking club. The most helpful single source of information about setting up a walking club comes from the Rockport Walking Institute. They have set up the Rockport Walk Leader Program and developed a comprehensive manual. The Rockport Walking Institute can be reached at 72 Howe Street, Marlborough, MA 01752.

Here are some tips to help you become a walk leader:

• Begin by explaining what fitness walking is and encouraging members to check with their physicians before beginning the program.

• Spend a meeting having the group take the Rockport Fitness Walking Test and finding their target heart rates. Show the members how to find their exercise program on the Rockport Fitness Walking Charts (Figure 1).

• To improve performance, introduce the members to the fitness-walking stride with good walking posture and swinging arms. Have the group warm up slowly to give the heart and lungs time to catch up.

• Divide the sessions into warm-up, stretch, aerobic training, cool-down, and stretch. If members vary in fitness, you will need to form more than one group for the walking part of the session.

• Explain safety precautions as you need them. Discuss hydration, safe and comfortable walking in heat and cold, and safety at night and in traffic.

• Plan indoor routes for times of extreme weather conditions so you will not have to cancel walking sessions.

• Keep a balance between the vigor of fitness walking and the fun of getting together with other people.

• Before people become bored, find a different route, plan a hike, set a destination—anything you can think of to vary the routine of your walks.

Encouraging members to persist through the first uncomfortable weeks may be your hardest job. As you know, it takes members eight to twelve weeks to begin to lose weight, tone their muscles, and feel more energetic. In the meantime many become tired at the end of each walk and wake up the next day with sore muscles. Help them by treating the completion of each walk as an accomplishment. Have a fifteen- to twenty-minute rest after the walk to give everybody time to catch their breath. Tell them how you felt when you began walking. Show them your logbook from the early days when you felt much as they do and encourage them to keep a walking log to record their progress.

Volksmarching

If you like the idea of more organized noncompetitive walking, you may be interested in a group called American Volkssport Association. This large international association organizes volksmarching, or "people walking," designed to appeal to people of all ages, especially to families. Volksmarching is based on the philosophy that people do not need to exercise in timed or competitive events. It promotes physical fitness and good health through exercise in a stress-free environment. Membership is not required and there is no minimum entry fee or any obligation to preregister for events. Volksmarching participants earn an event award for each walk they finish. Individuals are given achievement awards for the number of kilometers walked in those events, which take place all over the United States and in sixteen member countries.

Walks are typically ten kilometers (about six miles) long and explore scenic trails, river banks, historic sites, and downtown areas. Walking events may include more than one distance but always provide the minimum ten kilometers. You can finish events in two hours or longer, depending on your pace and how often you stop to enjoy the surroundings with your companions. For information write to AVA National Office, 1001 Pat Booker Road, Suite 203, Universal City, TX 78148.

Vacations for the Fitness Walker

"The food was great, but all we did was lie around. Now that vacation's over, I can get back in shape and take off these extra pounds."

"I really saw a lot—museums, monuments, beautiful buildings, and charming villages—and I learned a lot of history. But I didn't get to talk to people. I saw this old man out tending sheep. I'd like to have asked him about his sheepdog, but we just whizzed by in the car."

"Next time I want to take an active part in my vacation. I felt like an army recruit being moved from one place to another."

"Vacation turned out to be just as much of a hassle as the rest of the year. Next year I'm going to really get away from it all. Get back to nature."

If you have heard yourself or others making comments like this, you should think about a walking tour. As more and more people are discovering, a walking vacation improves your health while allowing an intimate look at a country's people, places, and culture.

WALKING ON YOUR OWN

If you enjoy making your own schedule, finding your own way, and working out your own travel arrangements, then touring on your own is for you. You choose your own time for leaving and can change your plans on a whim. A self-planned walking tour can be flexible enough to allow an extra day of travel if you want to linger, or to move on if you feel restless. You have freedom and independence no other vacation can match.

John Muir, the famous naturalist and walker who once rambled from Wisconsin to the Gulf of Mexico, described the minimal preparations he made for his trip: "I threw a loaf of bread and a pound of tea in an old sack and jumped over the back fence." For such a hardy soul as Muir, this might be the right attitude. But for the rest of us, following his example could lead to disaster. Successful walking trips begin for most people with good planning.

The first stops should be your local library and bookstore for maps and guidebooks. Look through the books with breathtaking pictures—they can help you choose a destination—but buy the ones with the latest and most detailed information; hiking maps and hiking guides are best. If you will be using a road map for walking, avoid the wide lines marked with the interstate shield symbol, which are the fastest, quickest routes. Instead, look for the small crooked roads or, better, the dotted lines that mark old logging trails or railway beds. If you are heading into wilderness or semi-wilderness, pick up topographical maps and study those contour lines marking elevations. They tell a lot about the difficulty of the route in terms of endurance and stamina.

Your research should include weather, accommodations, camping facilities, and tourist attractions. Chambers of Commerce, state tourist bureaus, and foreign tourist information offices are your best sources of information. A short list of sources is included in the Appendix of this book, but your local library can supply you with many more.

The French philosopher Jean Jacques Rousseau extolled the joys of a solitary walking tour: "Never did I think so much, exist so much, be myself so much as in the journeys I have made alone and on foot." Nevertheless such trips present problems. Planning can be fun, but nitty-gritty details are often frustrating, especially in foreign countries. Even making a hotel or airline reservation can be a time-consuming ordeal in some parts of the world. You are also responsible for transporting your own gear.

A final concern is safety. Studying guidebooks and maps can tell much about physical dangers; determining how the inhabitants will judge a solitary walker is more difficult. In some places, foreign and domestic walkers are an accepted part of the landscape. In others, a lone walker may be asking for trouble. The attentions of local men forced one experienced woman hiker to abandon her walking trip through Morocco. Another young hiker abandoned a tramp in Central America when one of his companions was threatened by drug dealers. You may not learn the ins and outs of safety from a state tourist bureau, but you probably can from a good guidebook. If possible, consult some people who have made the same trip.

The only way to experience many of the wilderness or semiwilderness areas is by backpacking, the most challenging kind of walking tour. You carry all you need to sustain you—food, shelter, and clothing—on your back. Armed with compass, topographical map, and sturdy walking shoes, backpackers venture into wilderness areas "in the raw," cooking their own food and sleeping in a sleeping bag under the stars. Light, reliable equipment is crucial on these off-road trips. Spend time choosing your most critical items: boots, pack, and sleeping bag. Lightweight gear has made all the difference in modern backpacking, but this kind of walking vacation is not for beginners. The weight of the pack, the demands of the trails, and the absence of amenities make it a real challenge.

The most popular backpacking areas in the United States are the lovely back country trails in the national parks and forests. Mountain routes that offer spectacular views, challenging terrain, and a sense of seclusion draw the most backpackers. Trails such as the 218-mile John Muir Trail in California, the 2,600-mile-long Pacific Crest Trail from Washington State to the California–Mexico border, the Mississippi to Ohio River Trail through southern Illinois, the Long Trail that runs the length of Vermont, the 2,100-mile Appalachian Trail from Maine to Georgia attract thousands of hikers and backpackers every year. Besides these famous trails, however, almost every state has parks and wilderness or semi-wilderness areas that are ideal for backpacking.

If you are organizing your own backpacking tour or adventure walk to a remote or primitive area of the world, be extra careful. Research your destination. Check weather, maps, terrain, and elevations, and study native culture so you know what to expect. Be sure you are in condition to handle long, arduous walks. Break in your shoes or boots and test all your gear—tent, rainwear, stove, and so on. Take enough equipment to make you self-reliant—clothing, food, stove, tent, and medical supplies including antibiotics. Get needed immunizations from your local hospital. The World Health Organization can tell you what shots you need if your doctor or hospital is unsure.

A variation on backpacking is carrying your pack but staying in lodgings along the way. This spares you the weight of your supplies and the effort of making camp. Gauge the distance of each day's walk to coincide with the availability of accommodations. This kind of walk keeps you closer to civilization than you would be on a full-fledged backpacking trip, making it ideal for touring country roads dotted with lovely villages and picturesque inns.

A third alternative is to select one hotel or guesthouse in a scenic area and use it as a base for walking trips in the vicinity. You won't have to carry a heavy pack or worry about accommodations. You won't cover as much territory, but you can enjoy the scenery and explore the countryside while you feel yourself growing stronger and healthier.

WALKING WITH AN ORGANIZED TOUR

If the problems of traveling on your own seem daunting, consider an organized walking tour. Walkers are usually a convivial band, and many people welcome the company and the camaraderie of those who share their love of walking. Though most organized walking tours allow for some variation in pace, group traveling necessarily circumscribes somewhat how long you can linger over the scenery or in a village.

An organized walking tour has many advantages. Experienced guides know the country and its people and are responsible for your safety. Your tour agency has your luggage driven to your destination each day. You get plenty of exercise while seeing the countryside, but you can relax in the evening while you enjoy a delightful dinner and comfortable lodgings. Best of all, the variety of trips to choose from is breathtaking. There are walking tour agencies in every state and almost every foreign country. Choosing which tour to take may be the hardest part.

On walking tours around the world, you traverse the countryside enjoying the scenery and chatting with fellow walkers and local people. All you carry is a day pack or a fanny pack to hold water and other necessities. Your tour agency tells you ahead of time how strenuous the walking is and what kind of gear you will need on any particular trip. Tours range from simple and cheap to luxurious and expensive, depending on your taste and pocketbook.

Though walking tours are not designed to test your stamina, groups generally cover between five and ten miles per day. To enjoy those miles you should be in good shape before you go on your vacation, so make sure you increase your daily walk to one hour, then longer until you feel capable of a ten-mile trek. If the trip you have signed on for leads through mountainous terrain, try to spend some time training in the mountains. Question your tour operator closely about the difficulty of the walks. "Challenging" could mean scaling a mountain and "good condition" may mean walking a seven-minute mile. Even if you are up for most challenges, be forewarned.

Don't worry too much about the pace of the group, however. Your tour guide explains the route each day and sets destinations along the way. Since everyone meets at the next destination, you determine your own pace and can find other members of the group to join you.

Once you have bought some good socks and broken in a pair of comfortable walking shoes or boots, the only rule to remember about gear is don't take much. Restricting yourself to one bag forces you to leave home stuff you have any doubts about bringing. Concentrate on casual, comfortable clothes, particularly items that approximate local dress. Rely on your tour operator for the best advice.

Before you sign on for a long walking tour, try several local overnight trips to be sure you really like the idea. Simply walking through a nearby state park and spending the night on the other side introduces you to the rhythm of a walking vacation. Take some friends along, so you can get the idea of hiking with a walking tour. For a more daring vacation, you might consider adventure walking. Porters or pack animals carry your gear, food, and equipment, while guides make camp, cook, and find the route. You can walk through wilderness or primitive countries in the four corners of the earth from Tibet or Nepal to Borneo or Brazil. Adventure walkers experience cultures and different people and test their mettle against the challenges of the wilderness. In remote regions where it is too dangerous or too difficult to walk alone, adventure tours have become increasingly popular.

WALKING IN THE CITY

Though to many people a walking vacation means walking through the countryside, seeing a city on foot gives you an opportunity to know the place in a way you never would through bus or car travel. To get really well acquainted with a city, walk around observing the shops, the schools, the little alleys and the broad avenues, people conducting business and strolling in the park. Look closely at those dramatic buildings and grand monuments. Almost every large city of Europe and America and many smaller ones in Europe and America have laid out walking tours that include all the major sights.

Washington, D.C., has a tour that begins at Blair House, goes by the Corcoran Art Gallery, the State Department, the Lincoln Memorial, the Jefferson Memorial, around the Tidal Basin and Washington Monument, down the Mall to the Capitol. Boston's Freedom Trail runs by the Old South Meeting House, the site of the Boston Massacre, Faneuil Hall, Paul Revere's house, and the Old North Church. Another tour cuts through Beacon Hill, the Boston Common, and Back Bay. A walking tour of San Francisco begins with a cable-car trip from Union Square through Nob Hill. The walk begins at Russian Hill, goes down the twisting Lombard Street and ends at Fisherman's Wharf.

In Rome one tour winds its way from the Pantheon, across the Tiber River, and past the Monument to Garibaldi, ending at St. Peter's. Another covers the seven hills of Rome and the Colosseum. In London a winding path leads from Piccadilly Circus down Regent's Street, through St. James's Park to the Houses of Parliament and Westminster Abbey, and from there to Buckingham Palace. Other walking tours cover the parts of London made famous in the novels of Dickens or Henry James. In Paris you can follow a tour that starts at the Grand Palais and progresses through the Tuileries Gardens, past the Louvre Museum to Notre Dame, through the Luxembourg Gardens, and back to the Louvre. All you need is the walking tour map from your hotel or a handy newsstand.

You can chart your own walking trip around a city by using a city map. Always keep in mind the main attractions you will want to see on your way. You can also trace the footsteps of historic figures, follow the banks of the Thames or the Seine, or poke into unexpected and interesting places. In between the museums, gardens, and historic sites, you'll meet Bostonians, New Yorkers, Romans, Dubliners, Londoners, and Parisians in shops, on street corners, and in parks.

APPENDIX: INFORMATION SOURCES*

Here is a list of associations, clubs, and organizations who can provide background information or answer questions about walking.

Walking Information

American Racewalk Assn.
P.O. Box 18323
Boulder, CO 80308-8323
(303) 447-0156
Viisha Sedlak, President

Established as a network for race walkers throughout the U.S. and to provide video coaching by mail, race-walk teaching standards, educational programs and materials, and discounted travel opportunities. An annual membership fee of $25 includes a welcome kit of instructional materials, and a quarterly newsletter with information on races, clinics, and camps.

American Volkssport Assn. (AVA)
1001 Pat Booker Rd.
Suite 203, Phoenix Square
University City, TX 78148
(512) 659-2112

Nonprofit organization sponsors noncompetitive family-oriented events in walking, bicycling, swimming, and cross-country skiing.

*Reprinted from *The Walking Magazine's* 1989 *Source Book,* © 1989, Raben Publishing Co., 711 Boylston Street, Boston, MA 02116

Canadian Volkssport Federation
La Fédération Canadienne Volkssport
National Office/Bureau National
P.O. Box 2668/C.P. 2668
Station "D"/Succursale "D"
Ottawa, Ont., Canada K1P 5W7

Nonprofit organization sponsors noncompetitive family-oriented events in walking, bicycling, swimming, and cross-country skiing.

Creative Walking Inc.
407-S. White Clay Center
Newark, DE 19711
(800) 762-9255 out of state
(302) 368-2222 in Delaware
Robert J. Sweetgall, President

Sponsors school, community, and corporate walking programs; leads seminars and workshops; publishes books.

Elderhostel
80 Boylston St., Suite 400
Boston, MA 02116
(617) 426-7788

A worldwide, nonprofit educational organization providing short-term, noncredit residential academic programs involving education and travel for people age 60 and over.

International Llama Assn.
P.O. Box 37505
Denver, CO 80237
(303) 699-9545

Provides llamas as trail companions for backpackers and hikers. Contact the association for a list of llama guides.

International Volkssportverband (IVV)
IVV-Schatzmeister Baldur Gerth
Alemannenstrasse 9,
D-6333 Braunfels
Bonabaden, West Germany
06442/22254

International organization made up of member clubs using the term *volkssports,* or popular sports, to describe noncompetitive walking, bicycling, and cross-country skiing events.

Keep Moving Program
Commonwealth of Massachusetts
Mass. Executive Office of Elder Affairs
38 Chauncy St.
Boston, MA 02111
(800) 882-2003 out of state
(617) 727-1108

Organizes statewide senior walking program and annual Governor's Cup event.

The 1988–89 National Directory of Walking Clubs
Raben Publishing Co.
711 Boylston St.
Boston, MA 02116
(617) 236-1885

An extensive list of more than 1,300 walking organizations, published in May 1988. Send check or money order for *The Walking Magazine*'s 1988 *Almanac,* $3.95.

National Organization of Mall Walkers (NOMW)
P.O. Box 191
Hermann, MO 65041
(314) 486-3945
Tom Cabot, Director

Offers mileage-incentive award program similar to AVA and President's Council on Physical Fitness. Individuals purchase log book from NOMW, walk a specific distance, and submit it for award. Membership available for individuals, clubs, and corporations. Members receive newsletters, discounts, and special incentives.

North American Racewalking Foundation
P.O. Box 50312
Pasadena, CA 91105
West Coast: Elaine Ward
(818) 577-2264
East Coast: John MacLachlan
(407) 393-6125

Nonprofit corporation founded to promote fitness and competitive race walking through sponsored events, clinics, and education.

Operation Lifestyle
Georgia Department of Human Resources
878 Peachtree Street, NE
Room 204
Atlanta, GA 30309
(404) 894-6589
Marsha Wilkinson, Director

Establishes walking programs for worksite and community groups.

PaceWalkers of America
Box QQ
East Setauket, NY 11733
Steven Jonas, M.D., Director

Founded to promote pace walking; offers free guides on how to start a walking club, and how to organize events.

Rockport Walking Institute
Box 480
Marlboro, MA 01752
(508) 485-2090

Subsidized wholly by The Rockport Co.; conducts and commissions research on walking and its cardiovascular benefits. Disseminates information through literature, forums, and events.

U.S. Orienteering Federation (USOF)
P.O. Box 1444
Forest Park, GA 30051
(404) 363-2110

A nonprofit organization for people interested in orienteering; *Orienteering North America,* an independently published magazine, featuring articles on improving skills, news updates, and events, is sent to all USOF members.

Walkabout International
835 Fifth Ave., Rm. 407
San Diego, CA 92101
(619) 231-SHOE (office)
(619) 223-WALK (tape)

Nonprofit group promotes neighborhood walking in urban, suburban, and rural environments. Sponsors variety of walks, publishes monthly schedule of events; maintains 24-hour hotline.

Walker's Club of America (WCA)
Box M
Livingston Manor, NY 12758
(914) 439-5155
Howard Jacobson, President

A network for walkers, WCA also conducts a summer training camp. For a list of walkers in your area and a suggested walking program, send a self-addressed stamped envelope.

Walking Assn.
P.O. Box 37228
Tucson, AZ 85740-7728
(602) 742-9589
Robert Sleight, Ph.D., Exec. Director

Nonprofit organization focuses on walker's rights, and promotional activities to enhance the quality of walking.

Walking for Wellness
Georgia Dept. of Human Resources and the Atlanta Regional Commission
878 Peachtree St., NE
Atlanta, GA 30309
(404) 894-6589
Ellen Smith, Director

Helps establish walking clubs in senior centers, retirement highrises, and aging programs; sponsors the annual Mayors' Walk for people 55 and over.

World Walkers Fellowship
1615 Enterprise Blvd.
Lake Charles, LA 70601
(318) 436-4897
Bud Deaton, President

Religious walking group organized to promote noncompetitive family-oriented events.

YMCA of the USA
101 N. Wacker Dr.
Chicago, IL 60606
(312) 977-0031
Cliff Lothery, Walking Director

Check with your local YMCA to see if it offers walking programs. There are some 2,200 YMCAs across the U.S. with a common mission of building a healthy body and spirit.

Hiking Information

Adirondack Mountain Club
R.D. 3, Box 3055
Luzerne Rd.
Lake George, NY 12845
(518) 793-7737
Walter M. Medwid, Exec. Director

Promotes conservation, education, and recreational activities aimed at protecting the Forest Preserve of New York State and encouraging outdoor recreational consistent with wilderness preservation. Open membership.

American Hiking Society (AHS)
1015 31st St., NW
Washington, DC 20007
(703) 385-3252
Susan A. Henley, Director

National nonprofit organization dedicated to protecting the interests of hikers and preserving America's footpaths. Over 70 club affiliates. Encourages volunteerism in trail-building and maintenance through work trips. Publishes "Volunteer Vacations" and directory of volunteer opportunities on public lands, "Helping Out in the Outdoors."

American Youth Hostels
National Office
P.O. Box 37613
Washington, DC 20013-7613
(202) 783-6161

Nonprofit membership organization provides hostel accommodations; educational, recreational, travel programs.

Appalachian Mountain Club (AMC)
5 Joy St. (Headquarters)
Boston, MA 02108
(617) 523-0636

Nonprofit hiking organization with 12 chapters and more than 35,000 members; outings, volunteer projects, monthly bulletin.

Florida Trail Assn. (FTA)
Rte. 1, Box 896 .
McAlpin, FL 32062
(904) 362-3256
Sylvia W. Dunnam, V.P.—Public Relations
Volunteer, nonprofit association dedicated to building hiking trails and educating members about careful usage and enjoyment of the outdoors.

Inland Empire Public Lands Council
P.O. Box 2174
Spokane, WA 99210

Publishes booklets of compiled newsclips on the politics of conservation.

North Country Trail Assn. (NCTA)
P.O. Box 311
White Cloud, MI 49349
(607) 272-8679
Thomas J. Reimers, Director

NCTA has accepted responsibility, in association with the National Park Service and other trail organizations, to build the 3,200-mile North Country Scenic Trail.

Pacific Northwest Trail Assn.
P.O. Box 1048
Seattle, WA 98111
(206) 827-7137
Ted Hitzroth, Director

Developers and protectors of the Pacific Northwest National Scenic Trail between the Continental Divide and the Pacific Ocean (Glacier National Park to Olympic National Park).

Sierra Club
730 Polk St.
San Francisco, CA 94109
(415) 776-2211
Victoria Wake, Director

Nonprofit membership organization works through grassroots activism, legislative action, and public education for conservation; offers large-scale local and national outings programs.

U.S. Dept. of Agriculture
Volunteers Program
Forest Service
Human Resource Programs
P.O. Box 37483
Washington, DC 20013
(202) 535-0920

Offers volunteer opportunities to work in national forests. For information and application, contact your regional Forest Service field office or national office listed above.

Women Outdoors
Curtis Hall
474 Boston Ave.
Medford, MA 02155

Nonprofit network of about 700 members nationwide who organize wilderness trips, workshops, and leadership seminars throughout the year.

Woodswomen
25 W. Diamond Lake Rd.
Minneapolis, MN 55419
(612) 822-3809
Denise Mitten, Executive Director

Organization for women who share an interest in outdoor activities, including mountaineering and backpacking. (Seattle Chapter, (206) 325-9589.)

Yellowstone Assn.
P.O. Box 117
Yellowstone Park, WY 82190
(307) 344-7381, ext. 2384
Jeanne Peterman, Director

Nonprofit educational group sponsors a large variety of summer field courses in Yellowstone. Including hiking, backpacking, and llama trekking; all classes involve field trips and walking.

Miscellaneous

American Heart Assn.
National Center
7320 Greenville Ave.
Dallas, TX 75231
(214) 373-6300

For American Heart Association–sponsored walks and informational materials on walking and cardiovascular health, the National Center suggests you contact your local organization.

American Running & Fitness Assn.
9310 Old Georgetown Rd.
Bethesda, MD 20814
(301) 897-0197

Nonprofit, educational association whose main goal is to educate the public about the benefits of a regular exercise program.

The Athletics Congress (TAC)
36 Canterbury Ln.
Mystic, CT 06355
Bruce Douglass, Chairman

National governing body for athletics in the United States

International Assn. for Medical Assistance to Travelers (IAMAT)
417 Center St.
Lewiston, NY 14092
(716) 754-4883

Nonprofit organization of overseas English-speaking doctors trained in the United States, Great Britain, and Canada providing medical assistance and information on food, water, diseases, and immunization to individuals traveling in other countries.

March of Dimes
1275 Mamaroneck Ave.
White Plains, NY 10606
(914) 428-7100

Birth-defects foundation sponsors national WalkAmerica, annual walkathon held the last weekend in April. For information, contact your local March of Dimes chapter.

President's Council on Physical Fitness & Sports
450 5th St., NW
Room 7103
Washington, DC 20001
(202) 272-3430
Steve GuBack, Director

Physical-fitness organization with a mission to be a catalyst in promoting the benefits of physical fitness for all segments of the population.

Rails-to-Trails Conservancy
1400 16th St., NW
Suite 300
Washington, DC 20036
(202) 797-5400

Keeps abreast of proposed railroad abandonment and publishes a manual to help the private sector convert railbeds to trails. Membership fee ($15 individual, $20 family) includes: newsletters, discounts on other publications, conferences, and workshops.

Women's Sports Foundation (WSF)
342 Madison Ave., Suite 728
New York, NY 10173
(800) 227-3988

Nonprofit, educational organization that serves as the national collective voice of all those who are dedicated to promoting and enhancing the sports experience for girls and women. By encouraging participation in sports, the WSF seeks to improve the physical, mental, and emotional well-being of all females.

State and Local Information

UNITED STATES

Alabama

Alabama Bureau of Tourism
532 Perry St.
Montgomery, AL 36104
(205) 261-4169
(800) 392-8096 in state
(800) 252-2262 out of state

Alaska

Alaska Div. of Tourism
Box E-101
Juneau, AK 99811
(907) 465-2010

Arizona

Arizona Office of Tourism
1480 E. Bethany Home Rd.
Phoenix, AZ 85014
(602) 255-3618

Arkansas

Arkansas Dept. of Parks & Tourism
One Capitol Mall
Little Rock, AR 72201
(800) 482-3999 in state
(800) 643-8383 out of state

California

California Dept. of Commerce
1121 L St., Suite 103
Sacramento, CA 95814
(916) 862-2543

Colorado

Colorado Tourism Board
5500 S. Syracuse Circle
Suite 267
Englewood, CO 80111
(800) 255-5550

Connecticut

Connecticut Dept. of Economic Devel.
210 Washington St.
Hartford, CT 06106
(203) 566-3948

Delaware

Delaware Tourism
P.O. Box 1401
Dover, DE 19903
(800) 282-8667 in state
(800) 441-8846 out of state

District of Columbia

Washington DC Convention & Visitors Assn.
1575 Eye St. NW
Washington, DC 20005
(202) 798-7000

Florida

Florida Div. of Tourism
126 W. Van Buren St.
Tallahassee, FL 32301
(904) 487-1462

Georgia

Georgia Dept. of Industry
Tourist Div.
P.O. Box 1776
Atlanta, GA 30301
(404) 656-3590

Hawaii

Hawaii Visitors Bureau
441 Lexington Ave., Suite 1407
New York, NY 10017
(808) 923-1811 in state
(212) 986-9203

Idaho

Idaho Travel Council
Department of Commerce
Statehouse
Boise, ID 83720
(208) 334-2470 in state
(800) 635-7820 out of state

Illinois

Illinois Office of Tourism
310 S. Michigan Ave.
Suite 108
Chicago, IL 60604
(312) 792-2094

Indiana	Indiana Tourism Development Div. One North Capitol, Suite 910 Indianapolis, IN 46204-2288 (317) 232-8860
Iowa	Iowa Tourism/Film Office 200 E. Grand Ave. Des Moines, IA 50309 (515) 281-3100
Kansas	Kansas Travel & Tourism Dept. of Commerce 400 W. 8th St. Topeka, KS 66603-3957 (913) 296-2009
Kentucky	Kentucky Dept. of Travel Devel. Capital Plaza Tower Frankfort, KY 40601 (502) 564-4930 in state (800) 225-8747
Louisiana	Louisiana Office of Tourism Box 94291 Capitol Sta. Baton Rouge, LA 70804 (504) 925-3860 in state (800) 334-8626 out of state
Maine	Maine Tourism Information Services 97 Winthrop St. Hallowell, ME 04347 (207) 289-2423
Maryland	Maryland Office of Tourist Devel. 45 Calvert St. Annapolis, MD 21401 (301) 974-3517
Massachusetts	Massachusetts Div. of Tourism 100 Cambridge St., 13th Fl. Boston, MA 02202 (617) 727-3201
Michigan	Michigan Travel Bureau Department of Commerce P.O. Box 30226 Lansing, MI 48909 (800) 543-2937

Minnesota	Minnesota Office of Tourism 375 Jackson St. 250 Skyway Level St. Paul, MN 55101 (800) 652-9747 in state (800) 328-1461 out of state Rovers, (612) 522-2461
Mississippi	Mississippi Div. of Tourism P.O. Box 849 Jackson, MS 39205-0849 (800) 962-2346 in state (800) 647-2290 out of state
Missouri	Missouri Div. of Tourism Truman Office Bldg. P.O. Box 1055 Jefferson City, MO 65102 (314) 751-4133
Montana	Travel Montana Dept. of Commerce Helena, MT 59620 (406) 444-4265 in state (800) 541-1447 out of state
Nebraska	Nebraska Div. of Travel & Tourism 301 Centennial Mall S P.O. Box 94666 Lincoln, NB 68509 (800) 742-7595 in state (800) 228-4307 out of state
Nevada	Nevada Commission on Tourism Capitol Complex Carson City, NV 89710 (702) 885-4322 in state (800) 638-2328 out of state
New Hampshire	New Hampshire Office of Vacation Travel P.O. Box 856 Concord, NH 03301 (603) 271-2666
New Jersey	New Jersey Travel & Tourism CN 826 Trenton, NJ 08625 (800) 537-7397

New Mexico	New Mexico Tourism & Travel Joseph M. Montoya Bldg. 1100 St. Francis Dr. Santa Fe, NM 87503 (505) 827-0291 in state (800) 545-2040 out of state
New York	New York State Dept. of Commerce One Commerce Plaza Albany, NY 12245 (518) 474-4116
North Carolina	North Carolina Div. of Travel & Tourism 430 N. Salisbury St. Raleigh, NC 27611 (919) 733-4171 in state (800) 847-4862 out of state
North Dakota	North Dakota Tourism Promotion Capitol Grounds Bismarck, ND 58505 (800) 472-2100 in state (800) 437-2077 out of state
Ohio	Ohio Div. of Travel & Tourism P.O. Box 1001 Columbus, OH 43266 (614) 466-8844 in state (800) 282-5393 out of state
Oklahoma	Oklahoma Tourism & Recreation 500 Will Rogers Bldg. Oklahoma City, OK 73105 (405) 521-2409
Oregon	Oregon Tourism 595 Cottage St. NE Salem, OR 97310 (800) 233-3306 in state (800) 547-7842 out of state
Pennsylvania	Pennsylvania Bureau of Travel Devel. 3200 S. 76th St. Philadelphia, PA 19153 (800) 847-4872

Rhode Island

Rhode Island Dept. of Economic Devel.
7 Jackson Walkway
Providence, RI 02903
(401) 277-2601

South Carolina

South Carolina Div. of Tourism
P.O. Box 71
Columbia, SC 29202
(803) 734-0122

South Dakota

South Dakota Div. of Tourism
Capitol Lake Plaza
Pierre, SD 57501-1000
(800) 952-2217 in state
(800) 843-1930 out of state

Tennessee

Tennessee Tourist Devel.
P.O. Box 23170
Nashville, TN 37202
(615) 741-2158 in state
(800) 221-2100 out of state

Texas

Texas Dept. of Highways
Travel Div.
11th & Brazos Sts.
Austin, TX 78701
(512) 465-7401

Utah

Utah Travel Council
Council Hall/Capitol Hill
Salt Lake City, UT 84114
(801) 538-1030

Vermont

Vermont Travel Div.
Montpelier, VT 05602
(802) 828-3236

Virginia

Virginia Div. of Tourism
202 N. 9th St., Suite 500
Richmond, VA 23219
(804) 786-4484

Washington

Washington Tourism Div.
101 General Admin. Bldg., AX-13
Olympia, WA 98504-0613
(800) 562-4570 in state
(800) 544-1800 out of state

West Virginia

West Virginia Dept. of Commerce
State Capitol
Charleston, WV 25305
(800) 225-5982

Wisconsin

Wisconsin Dept. of Devel.
Div. of Tourism
P.O. Box 7606
123 W. Washington Ave.
Madison, WI 53707
(608) 266-2161

Wyoming

Wyoming Travel Commission
Cheyenne, WY 82002
(307) 777-7777

CANADA

Alberta

Travel Alberta
Box 2500
Edmonton, Alta., Canada T5J 2Z4
(800) 661-8888

British Columbia

British Columbia Ministry of Tourism &
     Recreation
Parliament Bldgs.,
Victoria, B.C., Canada V8V 1X4

Manitoba

Manitoba Business Devel. & Tourism
Winnipeg, Man., Canada R3C 3H8
(800) 665-0040

New Brunswick

Tourism New Brunswick
P.O. Box 12345
Fredericton, N.B., Canada E3B 5C3

Newfoundland/Labrador

Newfoundland/Labrador Tourism
P.O. Box 2016
St. John's, Nfld., Canada A1C 5R8
(800) 563-6353

Northwest Territories

Northwest Territories Tourism Industry
     Assn.
Box 506
Yellowknife, N.W.T., Canada X1A 2N4

Nova Scotia	Nova Scotia Tourist Information Office 136 Commercial St. Portland, ME 04101 (800) 341-6096
Ontario	Ontario Ministry of Tourism Queen's Park Toronto, Ont., Canada M7A 2E5 (800) 268-3735
Prince Edward	Prince Edward Island Visitor Services P.O. Box 940 Charlottetown, P.E.I., Canada C1A 7M5
Quebec	Tourisme Quebec C.P. 20,000 Quebec, P.Q., Canada G1K 7X2 (800) 443-7000 eastern U.S. (418) 873-2015 elsewhere
Saskatchewan	Saskatchewan Tourism 2103 11th Ave. Regina, Sask., Canada S4P 3V7 (800) 667-7191

BIBLIOGRAPHY

Classic Hiking Books

The Art of Walking, ed. by Edwin Valentine Mitchell, New York, 1934. A collection of essays on walking by famous walkers.

The Footpath Way, An Anthology for Walkers, London, 1911. A collection of works about walking by famous people who loved walking—William Hazlitt, Henry David Thoreau, Robert Louis Stevenson, Sir Walter Scott, William Wordsworth, Walt Whitman, and others.

Excursions, Henry David Thoreau, New York, 1962.

A Thousand-Mile Walk to the Gulf, John Muir, New York, 1916.

The Appalachian Trail, Ann and Myron Sutton, New York, 1967.

The Man Who Walked Through Time, Colin Fletcher, New York, 1968.

The Complete Walker, Colin Fletcher, New York, 1984. Three volumes that are currently the most comprehensive guide to backpacking.

Trail Guides

Appalachian Mountain Club Guide to . . . The AMC has produced handy packets that include maps and pocket-size guidebooks to trails in many states.

The Sierra Club Guides to . . . The pocket-size Sierra Club guides describe hut-to-hut hikes in the United States and some in Europe.

INDEX